HEALTHY
VEGETARIAN
COOKERY

RECIPES FOR GOOD HEALTH

HEALTHY
VEGETARIAN
COOKERY

Written and compiled by
Nicole Oakley, SRD

OCTOPUS BOOKS

ACKNOWLEDGMENTS

The publisher acknowledges the following photographers: Rex Bamber page 117; Robert Golden page 116; Melvin Grey pages 23, 27, 40, 55, 63, 77, 82–3, 87, 91; Gina Harris page 97; Paul Kemp pages 31, 33, 48, 104–5; Norman Nicholls page 65; Roger Phillips pages 11, 18–19, 37, 45, 72, 95; Grant Symon cover, pages 2–3, 59, 112–13, 121; Paul Webster page 15; Paul Williams pages 50, 68–9. McDougalls Country Life Wholemeal Flour provided the photograph on page 101 and the Outline Slimming Bureau the photograph on page 80. Cookware, dishes and cutlery used in Grant Symon's photographs were provided by: Covent Garden Kitchen Supplies, 3 North Row, London WC2; Elizabeth David Ltd, 46 Bourne Street, London SW1; Graham and Green, 4 and 7 Elgin Crescent, London W11; David Mellor, 4 Sloane Square, London, SW1, 26 James Street, Covent Garden, London WC2 and 66 King Street, Manchester M2; and Wilson and Gill, 137 Regent Street, London, W1. The author wishes to thank Betty Lammin. Alex Gray-Muir, Francesca Oakley and Diane Stillman for their recipe suggestions.

Line drawings by Alun Jones.

Cover illustration (clockwise from top): Avocado, grapefruit and sesame salad (page 32), Summer pudding (page 93), Broccoli pancakes (page 45), Mixed cheese and herbs (page 81). Title spread illustration: Hazelnut and raspberry torte (page 99), Courgettes provençales (page 67).

COOKING NOTE

The measurements in the recipes are given in both metric and imperial units. Use whichever system you are familiar with, but do not mix the two as the equivalents are not exact.

When spoonfuls are mentioned use level spoons:
1 teaspoon = 5 ml
1 tablespoon = 15 ml.

Australian readers who use a 20 ml tablespoon should use 3 × 5 ml teaspoons to get the correct measure for the recipes in this book.

The labels on the recipes are to be interpreted as follows:

High-fibre These high-fibre recipes contain at least 3 g fibre in each portion – around one tenth of your daily target. They will help you to increase your daily fibre intake.

Low-fat This indicates that less than 35 per cent of the calories are derived from fat.

Vegan This indicates that the dish is suitable for vegans, and contains no products of animal origin.

FOR NIGEL

A Ridgmount book

This edition first published 1986 by
Octopus Books Ltd
59 Grosvenor Street, London W1

© 1986 Octopus Books Ltd

ISBN 0 7064 2623 1

Printed in Hong Kong

CONTENTS

Healthy Vegetarian Eating

More than ever before, an increasing number of people are turning to a vegetarian diet. In fact, a recent Gallup poll has revealed that almost 3 million people in Britain (over 16 per cent of the adult population) have either eliminated red meat from their diets or have become vegetarians. Whether for ethical or ecological reasons or as a matter of taste, there is growing awareness that a vegetarian diet is a sound basis for healthy eating.

In this book, I have tried to combine the principles of eating for good health with recipes for interesting food.

A vegetarian diet can be tailored to everyone's needs and tastes. Many people first just cut down on the amount of meat they eat – particularly expensive red meat – and increase their intake of vegetables, fruit and bread. This can be done gradually or at a quicker pace if your tastebuds and habits become accustomed to it.

Eventually you may want to adhere more strictly to vegetarian principles. Here, too, there is a variety of diets from which to choose. All vegetarians avoid meat, fish and fowl and any products from these, such as suet, dripping, gelatine and meat extracts. In addition, lacto-vegetarians eat dairy products (cheese, milk, yogurt and so on), while ovo-lacto-vegetarians also include eggs in their diets. The strictest vegetarians of all – called vegans – eat nothing that comes from animals.

WHAT IS A HEALTHY DIET?

Recent medical reports have examined the role of diet in the cause of disease and in its prevention. They have concluded that, in developed countries, a substantial number of people are overweight, a condition associated with an increased risk of developing diabetes, heart disease and high blood pressure.

In addition it is suggested that many of us consume too much alcohol, take too high a proportion of our calories in the form of fats and oils, and do not consume enough fibre, or "roughage". And many people also eat too much sugar and salt.

The reports' recommendations are mainly designed to help keep weight down within normal limits. The best way to achieve this is by taking regular exercise and reducing the amount of fat and sugar that you eat. Bear in mind too that alcohol is also high in calories.

Vegetarian diets may aid weight control as they tend to be bulky so that you feel satisfied without taking too many calories.

FIBRE

Dietary fibre, or "roughage", is the indigestible outer skins and cell walls of a whole range of plants. There are two types: WATER-INSOLUBLE FIBRE passes through the intestines without being absorbed. This increases the bulk in the large intestine, which makes the stools softer and thus easier to pass, so preventing constipation. WATER SOLUBLE FIBRE found mostly in pulses, slows down the rate of absorption of sugars such as glucose, and may be of marginal benefit in the management of diseases in which the levels of sugar or cholesterol in the blood are too high – for example, diabetes. It is thought that certain other diseases may also be avoided by eating enough fibre; these include diverticular disease of the intestines, appendicitis, varicose veins, piles (haemorrhoids), bowel cancer and gallstones.

The main sources of fibre are the wholegrain cereals and cereal products, such as wholemeal flour and foods made from it. Varying amounts of fibre are also found in such protein sources as pulses, seeds, nuts as well as in unpeeled potatoes and other vegetables and in fruit. Some vitamins and minerals as well as fibre are lost during the milling of white flour, although some of the former are replaced by manufacturers. All breads provide valuable protein.

Crude miller's bran, the outer husk of wheat that is removed during milling, is sometimes advocated as a laxative. However, the introduction of relatively large amounts of this on its own into the diet is not advisable, for along with the bran comes phytic acid, a substance that combines with minerals (especially zinc, calcium and iron) and renders them unavailable to the body. The bran in wholemeal bread does not cause this problem to the same extent, as the yeast provides enzymes to counteract the effect.

FATS

Too much fat is bad for you, and you should focus on increasing your consumption of unrefined carbohydrates – that is, foods such as cereals, bread, rice and root vegetables – as well as fruit and other vegetables, at the expense of fat-rich items. Most people should reduce the amount of fat they eat by a quarter, until it is no more than 35 per cent of their daily energy (calorie) intake.

Less than half of the fat you eat should be in the form of saturated (animal) fat. Saturated fat can be identified in most instances because it solidifies at room temperature. Thus, most animal fats – such as lard, butter and the obvious as well as the "invisible" fat on meat – are saturated while most of the vegetable oils are unsaturated and remain liquid. Choose a margarine that is high in polyunsaturated fat. (Vegans, of course, will choose margarines without added animal fats and should substitute these for the polyunsaturated margarines in the recipes.)

Although you shouldn't overindulge in eating fats, you do need to eat some if you are to remain healthy. Polyunsaturated fats provide linoleic acid, an essential fatty acid that the body needs but cannot make itself, so it has to be found in the food we eat. Fats also provide a medium for the transport of the fat-soluble vitamins A and D.

Vegetarians start with an advantage because they already avoid animal foods, which are the main source of the unwanted saturated fats. Nevertheless, all types of fat provide around twice as many calories, gram for gram, as the other main constituents of food – protein and carbohydrate – and your total intake must be kept in check if you are going to keep your weight under control.

The main sources of fat in vegetarian diets are dairy products, margarine, oils and nuts. There are a number of ways to avoid fats and still have appetizing meals.

MILK AND YOGURT Half a pint (300 ml) of whole milk a day provides you with 80 g of fat a week. Try substituting skimmed milk, which is devoid of fat but still contains important minerals and B vitamins. If the taste is unacceptable, start by using semi-skimmed milk on cereals and in tea and coffee, and skimmed milk in cooking. Natural low-fat yogurt usually contains about 1 per cent fat, though some brands contain as much as 10 per cent. Yogurt can replace cream as a topping, and if drained through muslin for several hours, will thicken sufficiently to be piped or used as curd cheese.

CHEESES Hard cheeses, such as Cheddar, contain 50 per cent more fat than softer ones such as Camembert and Edam. You will use less if you grate it and mix this with such things as peeled tomatoes. There are now also fat-reduced Cheddar cheeses on the market. Soft cheeses (and polyunsaturated margarines and low-fat spreads) are easier to spread and can therefore be used more sparingly. Avoid spreading fats on hot bread or toast, as far more is used this way. Use low-fat soft cheeses such as "quark" instead of cream cheese.

EGGS Keep your egg intake down to three or four a week. As the fat is contained only in the yolk, whites do not need to be restricted, and they can usefully add volume to a dish, such as in the Cheese soufflé.

SALAD DRESSINGS Using oils with interesting tastes, like walnut or sesame seed, means less is needed. A wine vinegar, like balsamic vinegar, is less sharp, so the proportion of vinegar to oil can be increased; you can also add water without detracting from the taste. The oil in mayonnaise can be reduced if a cornflour base is used (as in Watercress mayonnaise), or the mayonnaise can be mixed with low-fat yogurt.

NUTS With the exception of chestnuts, which are low in fat, between 35 and 50 per cent of the weight of nuts is fat, although it is mostly unsaturated (except in the case of coconuts). Nuts are a good protein source and can therefore be seen as an alternative to cheese, which contains saturated fat.

COOKING HINTS When baking, use non-stick cake tins, or line tins with silicone-treated paper. By frying in a non-stick pan you can reduce the amount of oil needed for cooking. If oil is required, apply it sparingly with a pastry brush.

Rather than having fat-rich pastry, choose dessert recipes using bread as a base, such as Summer pudding, and substitute filo or Strudel paste for flaky or shortcrust pastry. Cobblers also call for less fat in the topping.

	FOODS HIGH IN FAT	FAT %	ALTERNATIVES	FAT %
CHEESE	Cheddar and similar hard cheeses	34	Reduced-fat Cheddar and Cheshire cheese	15
	Camembert	23		
	Cream cheese	47	Cottage cheese	4
	Edam/cheese spread	22		
	Parmesan	30		
	Stilton	40		
MILK AND MILK PRODUCTS	Whole milk	4	Skimmed milk	0·1
			Semi-skimmed	1·5
	Double cream	48	Yogurt	1·0
	Ice cream	7		
FATS (eating)	Butter and margarine	85	Low-fat spread	40
OILS	All types	100		
FRUIT	Avocado pears	22	All other fruits	Trace only
	Olives	8		
NUTS AND SEEDS	Almonds, brazils and walnuts	50	Chestnuts	2
	Hazelnuts	36		
	Coconut (fresh)	36		
	Coconut (desiccated)	62		
	Peanut butter	53		
	Sesame seeds	54		
VEGETABLES	Potato chips	18	Jacket potatoes	0·1
	Potato crisps	35		

SUGAR

People in developed countries eat far too much sugar. Every year the British consume an average of 38 kg of sugar per person. The term "sugar" covers white and brown sugars (sucrose) and other simple sugars such as maltose, glucose and lactose, which are often added to manufactured goods as diverse as cola drinks, tomato ketchup and tinned meats.

Sugar provides nothing of nutritional value, and an excess should be avoided. The best way of doing this is by gradually reducing the amount of sweet foods and drinks. Substitute fresh fruit for sugar, fat-rich cakes and biscuits. If you still crave a sweet taste, add dried fruits – apricots, prunes, sultanas, raisins – to food instead of sugar. These natural sources of sweetness not only taste good, but also provide fibre and iron.

SALT

Modern methods mean that sodium chloride is no longer essential as a preservative, yet salt is still consumed in large amounts, despite the fact that high intakes have been implicated in the development of high blood pressure. Although salt is an essential constituent of the diet, the needs of the body can be met by one-tenth of what the average person usually consumes. The palate can gradually be educated to prefer a less salty taste by cutting down its use in food preparation and at the table. Introduce more herbs and spices into your cooking to provide alternative flavours.

You can also avoid salty foods – for example, eat unsalted rather than salted peanuts. Check the labels on manufactured items, and if sodium in any of its various forms is mentioned, be careful.

COOKING VEGETABLES

The vitamins in freshly picked vegetables are easily lost during storage, preparation and cooking. Vegetables should be prepared just before being cooked, and then plunged into a minimum of boiling water. To preserve the vitamin C, which is easily oxidized, always put a lid on the pan. Cook for as short a time as possible – 5 to 10 minutes – to minimize the destruction of heat-sensitive vitamins, and serve at once.

THE GOLDEN RULES

The main points to remember when planning a healthy vegetarian diet are:

1 Eat whole-grain cereals and products made from them.

2 Eat plenty of vegetables and use pulses as a low-fat protein source.

3 Be alert to the foods that contain fat and only eat small portions of them.

4 Eat low-fat yogurt, cottage cheese, soft cheeses and skimmed milk.

5 Use polyunsaturated margarines in preference to butter.

6 Use soya, corn or sunflower oils in cooking, mixing these with olive, walnut or sesame seed oils for salads.

7 Keep your egg intake down to three or four a week.

8 Eat fruit for desserts.

9 Cook vegetables in the minimum amount of water for the minimum amount of time.

10 Restrict your consumption of commercially prepared foods, which usually contain large quantities of saturated fats, sugar and salt.

11 Try to limit your intake of alcohol to not more than one or two drinks a day. Too much alcohol is bad for you and also greatly increases your daily calorie intake.

12 Vegans should ensure an adequate daily intake of vitamin B_{12}, either from supplements or vitamin B_{12} fortified foods.

13 To ensure perfect protein balance, vegans should combine a cereal-based food with a seed or nut dish, twice daily.

Breakfast Recipes

MUESLI

225 g / 8 oz rolled oats
225 g / 8 oz barley flakes or kernels and
  wheatgerm, mixed according to taste
50 g / 2 oz mixed nuts, chopped
50 g / 2 oz seedless raisins and coarsely chopped
  dried fruit (apples, apricots, dates, figs),
  mixed according to taste

MAKES 500 g / 1¼ lb
Low Fat   High Fibre   Vegan

Put the oats in a bowl, then stir in the remaining ingredients. Store in a tin or other airtight container and use as required.

Serve with fruit juice or plain unsweetened yogurt. Fresh fruit may be added according to season.

FRUIT MUESLI WITH YOGURT

100 g / 4 oz rolled oats
4 tablespoons wheatgerm
2 tablespoons skimmed milk powder
450 ml / ¾ pint skimmed milk
50 g / 2 oz prunes, stoned and chopped
50 g / 2 oz stoned dates, chopped
25 g / 1 oz seedless raisins
25 g / 1 oz walnuts, chopped
1 orange, peel and pith removed and divided
  into segments

1 grapefruit, peel and pith removed and divided
  into segments
100 g / 4 oz grapes, halved and seeded
300 ml / ½ pint plain unsweetened yogurt
  (optional)

SERVES 4
Low Fat   High Fibre

Put the oats into a bowl, add the wheatgerm, milk powder, milk, dried fruit and nuts and stir well to mix. Cover and leave in the refrigerator overnight.

The next morning, divide the muesli equally between four individual serving bowls, then arrange the prepared fruit on top. Top with yogurt, if liked.

FRUIT MUESLI WITH YOGURT

BANANA FLIP

4 bananas, peeled and sliced
600 ml / 1 pint skimmed milk
225 g / 8 oz cottage cheese
pinch of ground cinnamon

SERVES 4
Low Fat

Put the bananas and milk into a blender and blend for 30 seconds. Add the cottage cheese and blend for a further 30 seconds.

Pour into chilled glasses and sprinkle with cinnamon. Serve immediately.

WHOLEMEAL SODA BREAD

225 g / 8 oz plain wholemeal flour
225 g / 8 oz plain flour
1 teaspoon salt
2 teaspoons bicarbonate of soda
2 teaspoons cream of tartar

50 g / 2 oz polyunsaturated margarine, cut into pieces
300 ml / ½ pint buttermilk or soured milk

MAKES 1 × 450 g (1 lb) loaf

This bread is best eaten on the day it is made, as it goes stale very quickly. Fresh skimmed milk with a teaspoon of lemon juice can be substituted for soured milk.

Grease a baking sheet. Sift the flours together into a warm mixing bowl with the salt, bicarbonate of soda and cream of tartar. Return the bran to the sifted ingredients. Rub in the margarine, then bind the mixture together with the buttermilk or soured milk.

Shape the dough into a round and place it on the baking sheet. Slash the surface with a sharp knife, sprinkle the surface with flour and bake in a preheated hot oven (220°C, 425°F, Gas Mark 7) for about 25 minutes. Turn out and cool on a wire tray.

HOT APPLE MUFFINS

225 g / 8 oz plain wholemeal flour
pinch salt
1 tablespoon baking powder
50 g / 2 oz caster sugar
2 eggs
150 ml / ¼ pint skimmed milk

50 g / 2 oz polyunsaturated margarine, melted
75 g / 3 oz dessert apples, peeled and grated

MAKES 20–24 muffins
Low Fat   High Fibre

Sift together the dry ingredients in a mixing bowl and return the bran in the sieve to the flour. In another bowl beat the eggs, add the milk and melted margarine. Stir the liquid very quickly into the flour mixture. Do not beat and do not worry about lumps – speed is essential. Fold in the grated apples. Fill 5 cm (2 inch) greased bun tins or paper cases to one-third full.
Bake in a preheated hot oven (220°C, 425°F, Gas Mark 7) for 15–25 minutes, until cooked. Remove from tins or cases and serve hot.

FRENCH TOAST

4 slices slightly stale wholemeal bread, crusts
  removed
250 ml/8 fl oz skimmed milk
1 egg, lightly beaten

2 teaspoons caster sugar mixed with a good
  pinch of cinnamon

MAKES 4 slices

Lay the bread in a shallow dish. Whisk the milk into the egg and pour over the bread.

Leave to soak for a few minutes, then turn over and allow the mixture to soak well into the bread.

Brush a large non-stick frying pan with a little oil and cook the bread until golden brown, turn the slices and brown the other side. Sprinkle with the caster sugar and serve at once.

PORRIDGE

175 g/6 oz coarse or medium oatmeal, or rolled
  or jumbo oats
1.2 litres/2 pints water
1 teaspoon salt (optional)

SERVES 4
Low Fat   High Fibre

If preferred, the oats can be soaked in the water overnight and the cooking time reduced to about 5 minutes.

Place the oatmeal or oats in a saucepan with the water and bring to the boil. Add the salt, if used, cover and simmer gently for 15–20 minutes, stirring frequently. Serve with a little honey, molasses or muscovado sugar and semi-skimmed or soya milk if desired.

Soups
& Starters

FRESH TOMATO SOUP

1 tablespoon vegetable oil
1 large onion, peeled and finely chopped
2 garlic cloves, crushed
450 g/1 lb ripe tomatoes, skinned and chopped
300 ml/½ pint Vegetable stock (page 20)
2 sprigs fresh basil, chopped
salt and freshly ground black pepper

TO GARNISH
2 sprigs parsley, chopped

SERVES 4
Low Fat   Vegan

Heat the oil in a large saucepan and fry the onions and garlic gently. Add the tomatoes to the onions with the Vegetable stock, basil, salt and pepper to taste.

Simmer for 10 minutes and serve sprinkled with chopped parsley.

GAZPACHO

700 g/1½ lb tomatoes, skinned, seeded and
   chopped
1 × 10 cm/4 inch piece of cucumber, chopped
1 onion, peeled and finely chopped
½ green pepper, cored, seeded and chopped
2 garlic cloves, peeled
1 tablespoon vegetable oil
3 tablespoons lemon juice
1 teaspoon chopped thyme
2 tablespoons chopped parsley
salt and freshly ground black pepper

iced water
TO GARNISH
ice cubes
½ green pepper, cored, seeded and finely diced
1 × 10 cm/4 inch piece of cucumber, finely
   chopped
4 celery sticks, trimmed and finely chopped
finely chopped parsley

SERVES 4
Low Fat   Vegan

Put the tomatoes, cucumber, onion, green pepper, garlic, oil, lemon juice, parsley, thyme, salt and pepper into a blender and work to a purée.

Add enough iced water to make the soup of the desired consistency. The quantity will vary according to the juiciness of the tomatoes, and your preference for a really thick or a thin soup.

Chill thoroughly. Float an ice cube in each serving and hand round the garnishes in separate bowls.

MUSHROOM SOUP

MUSHROOM SOUP

350 g / 12 oz dark mushrooms, trimmed and
  finely chopped
1 onion, peeled and sliced
300 ml / ½ pint Vegetable stock (page 20)
25 g / 1 oz polyunsaturated margarine
25 g / 1 oz plain wholemeal flour
600 ml / 1 pint skimmed milk
6 tablespoons medium sherry
salt and freshly ground black pepper

6 tablespoons plain unsweetened yogurt
TO GARNISH
50 g / 2 oz button mushrooms, trimmed and
  thinly sliced
1 tablespoon chopped fresh parsley

SERVES 4
Low Fat

Put the mushrooms and onion in a pan
with the stock and bring to the boil then
cover the pan and simmer for 20 minutes.

Sieve the mushroom mixture, or purée
in a blender or food processor. Set aside.

Melt the margarine in the saucepan, stir
in the flour and cook for 1 minute. Pour on
the milk slowly, stirring all the time. Bring
to the boil, stirring, then simmer for 3
minutes. Stir in the mushroom purée and
sherry, and season to taste with salt and
pepper. Bring to the boil again, stir in the
yogurt and heat through without boiling.

Ladle the soup into individual bowls.
Float the sliced mushrooms on top and
sprinkle with the parsley.

VEGETABLE BORTSCH

1 tablespoon oil
1 onion, peeled and sliced
1.75 litres/3 pints water
500 g/1¼ lb beetroot, peeled and roughly
    chopped
1 large carrot, scraped and chopped
2 celery sticks, trimmed and chopped
salt and freshly ground black pepper
225 g/8 oz cabbage, trimmed and shredded

2 garlic cloves, peeled and chopped
2 tablespoons tomato purée
1 tablespoon lemon juice
1 tablespoon chopped parsley
150 ml/¼ pint plain unsweetened yogurt

SERVES 8
Low Fat

Heat the oil in a large pan, add the onion and fry until softened, about 5 minutes. Add the water, beetroot, carrot, celery and salt and pepper to taste. Bring to the boil, cover and simmer over a low heat for 30 minutes. Add the cabbage, garlic and tomato purée, and simmer for 20 minutes.

Add the lemon juice and parsley, blending well. Adjust the seasoning. Pour into individual serving bowls and swirl the yogurt over the top. Serve immediately.

FRENCH ONION SOUP

3 tablespoons vegetable oil
500 g/1¼ lb onions, peeled and thinly sliced
1 tablespoon plain flour
1.2 litres/2 pints Vegetable stock (page 20)
1 bouquet garni

salt and freshly ground black pepper
4–5 slices French bread, 1 cm/1 inch thick
25 g/1 oz Gruyère cheese, grated

SERVES 4

Heat the oil in a large saucepan, add the onions and fry gently, stirring occasionally, for 10–15 minutes until golden. Stir in the flour, then gradually add the stock, stirring constantly. Add the bouquet garni and salt and pepper to taste. Cover and simmer for about 30 minutes.

Toast the thick slices of French bread

lightly on both sides.

Ladle the soup into individual flameproof bowls and place a piece of toast on each one. Sprinkle with the cheese and place under a hot grill until golden brown and bubbling.

CARROT AND GINGER SOUP

350 g/12 oz carrots, scraped and sliced
600 ml/1 pint Vegetable stock (page 20)
1 piece fresh root ginger, peeled
25 g/1 oz polyunsaturated margarine
2 medium onions, peeled and sliced
1 teaspoon ground ginger
1 teaspoon grated orange rind
2 tablespoons orange juice

salt and freshly ground black pepper
TO GARNISH
4 tablespoons plain unsweetened yogurt
4 small sprigs fresh parsley

SERVES 4
Low Fat

Put the carrots, stock and ginger into a pan. Bring to the boil and simmer for 15 minutes. Discard the ginger and remove and reserve 1 tablespoon of the carrot slices.

Melt the margarine in a saucepan, add the onions and fry gently for 3 minutes. Stir in the ground ginger and cook for 1 minute. Stir in the orange rind and juice and add the carrots and stock. Cover the pan, bring to the boil and simmer for 10 minutes.

Purée the soup in a blender or food processor, or rub through a sieve. Return the purée to the pan and season to taste with salt and pepper.

To make the garnish, thinly slice the reserved carrot slices and stamp out shapes with aspic cutters.

Reheat the soup. Pour into a heated tureen or individual bowls. Swirl on the yogurt and garnish with the carrot shapes and parsley sprigs.

NETTLE SOUP

450 g/1 lb potatoes, peeled and thickly sliced
salt
15 g/½ oz polyunsaturated margarine
225 g/8 oz young nettles, washed, trimmed and
    chopped
900 ml/1½ pints Vegetable stock (page 20)

freshly ground black pepper
4 tablespoons plain unsweetened yogurt

SERVES 4
Low Fat

Make this soup in the spring when the nettles are very young and tender and only use the top 5 cm/2 inch of the nettles. Wear thick gloves when gathering nettles.

Cook the potatoes for 10 minutes in salted water and drain.

Melt the margarine in a saucepan, add the nettles, cover and stew gently for 10 minutes. Add the parboiled potatoes and the stock, bring to the boil, and simmer for another 10 minutes until the potatoes are soft. Cool slightly, then purée in a blender and return the soup to the rinsed-out pan. Add salt and pepper to taste and stir in the plain yogurt.

CHILLED WATERCRESS VICHYSSOISE

15 g/½ oz polyunsaturated margarine
1 large onion, peeled and chopped
225 g/8 oz leeks, trimmed and sliced
350 g/12 oz potatoes, peeled and diced
1 litre/1¾ pints Vegetable stock (page 20)
grated rind of ½ lemon

salt and freshly ground black pepper
2 bunches watercress, trimmed
150 ml/¼ pint skimmed milk

SERVES 6
Low Fat

Melt the margarine in a large saucepan and cook the onion and leeks gently for 5 minutes, stirring constantly. Add the potatoes to the pan and pour in the stock with the lemon rind, and salt and pepper.

Cover the pan and bring to the boil. Simmer for 30 minutes until the vegetables are tender.

Reserve a few sprigs of watercress and coarsely chop the rest. Add the chopped watercress to the pan and simmer for 2 minutes.

Liquidize to a smooth purée. Stir in the milk and taste and adjust the seasoning. Chill well before serving. Garnish with the reserved watercress.

ICED AVOCADO SOUP

2 ripe avocados, halved and stoned
2 teaspoons lemon juice
1 celery stick, very finely chopped
1 tablespoon tomato purée
450 ml / ¾ pint plain unsweetened yogurt
300 ml / ½ pint Vegetable stock (page 20)

1–2 drops Tabasco sauce
salt and freshly ground black pepper
TO GARNISH
chopped chives

SERVES 4

Do not prepare this soup more than an hour before you intend to serve it, as the avocados may discolour.

Spoon the avocado flesh into a bowl, add the lemon juice and beat to a smooth paste. Beat in the celery, tomato purée, yogurt, Tabasco, and salt and pepper. Add sufficient Vegetable stock to obtain a thick but liquid soup, then adjust the seasoning. Chill in the refrigerator, resting the bowl on a bed of ice to hasten the chilling process. Serve garnished with chives.

LEFT: MINESTRONE; RIGHT: CHILLED PEA SOUP

CHILLED PEA SOUP

350 g/12 oz shelled peas (about 750 g/1½ lb fresh peas in the pod)
1 onion, peeled and chopped
1 large mint sprig
finely grated rind and juice of ½ lemon
900 ml/1½ pints Vegetable stock (page 20)
salt and freshly ground black pepper

150 ml/¼ pint plain unsweetened yogurt, or skimmed milk
TO GARNISH
1 tablespoon chopped mint

SERVES 6
Low Fat   High Fibre

Put the peas in a pan with the onion, mint, lemon rind and juice, stock and salt and pepper to taste.

Bring to the boil, then lower the heat, cover and simmer for 30 minutes until the peas are soft. Work the soup to a purée through a sieve or in a blender. Leave to cool completely.

Stir in the yogurt or milk, taste and adjust seasoning, then chill until required in the refrigerator.

Sprinkle with chopped mint and serve chilled.

MINESTRONE

1 onion, peeled and sliced
1 garlic clove, peeled and crushed (optional)
1 carrot, scraped and diced
1 turnip, peeled and diced
1 leek, trimmed and sliced
1 celery stick, trimmed and sliced
225 g/8 oz tomatoes, skinned and roughly chopped
50 g/2 oz broken wholemeal pasta or long-grain brown rice
1.2 litres/2 pints Vegetable stock (page 20)
salt and freshly ground black pepper
¼ small cabbage, trimmed and shredded
100 g/4 oz runner beans, trimmed and sliced

SERVES 6
Low Fat   High Fibre   Vegan

Put the onion, garlic, if used, carrot, turnip, leek, celery, tomatoes and pasta or rice into a large pan. Stir in the stock and add salt and pepper to taste.

Bring to the boil, then lower the heat, cover and simmer for 30 minutes until the vegetables are tender.

Add the cabbage and beans and cook for a further 5–10 minutes until tender. Taste and adjust seasoning, then serve hot with Parmesan cheese either handed separately or sprinkled on top of each bowl.

GREEK VEGETABLE SOUP

450 ml / ¾ pint Vegetable stock (page 20)
100 g / 4 oz frozen mixed vegetables
1 egg yolk
300 ml / ½ pint plain unsweetened yogurt
salt and freshly ground black pepper

1 tablespoon chopped fresh mint
grated rind of 1 lemon

SERVES 4

Put the stock into a saucepan and bring to the boil. Add the vegetables and simmer for 5 minutes.

Lightly beat the egg yolk with the yogurt in a bowl. Add about 6 tablespoons of the hot stock and mix well, then stir this into the soup and heat through gently without boiling. Season to taste with salt and pepper.

Ladle the soup into individual bowls and sprinkle the mint and lemon rind on top. Serve hot.

VEGETABLE STOCK

2 tablespoons vegetable oil
450 g / 1 lb onions, peeled and sliced
450 g / 1 lb carrots, scraped and sliced
1 head celery, trimmed, with the leaves, roughly
    chopped
1.75 litres / 3 pints water

1 bouquet garni
6 white peppercorns
½ teaspoon salt

MAKES 1.5 litres / 2½ pints
Low Fat   Vegan

Heat the oil in a large pan, add the vegetables and fry gently until softened, stirring frequently. Do not allow the vegetables to become browned or this will spoil the colour of the finished stock.

Stir in the water, then add the remaining ingredients and bring slowly to the boil. Lower the heat, skim off any scum with a slotted spoon, then half-cover with a lid. Simmer for 1–2 hours. Top up the water during the cooking time if the liquid reduces more than a little in the pan.

Tip the contents of the pan into a sieve or fine colander lined with muslin wrung out in hot water. Press firmly to extract as much stock as possible.

Leave the stock until completely cold. Cover and store in the refrigerator for up to 5 days, or in the freezer for up to 3 months. Bring to the boil before using as required.

VINE-LEAF PARCELS

2 × 225 g (8 oz) canned or bottled vine leaves,
    drained
salt
½ teaspoon ground turmeric
175 g / 6 oz long-grain brown rice
1 tablespoon vegetable oil
1 small onion, peeled and finely chopped
100 g / 4 oz dried apricots, finely chopped
50 g / 2 oz sultanas

pinch of ground cinnamon
pinch of ground allspice
1 tablespoon chopped fresh mint
1 teaspoon lemon juice
300 ml / ½ pint unsweetened orange juice
150 ml / ¼ pint water

SERVES 4
Low Fat   High Fibre   Vegan

Unroll the vine leaves carefully and put them into a bowl of water to remove the preserving liquid. Pat them dry on absorbent kitchen paper. You will need about 30 leaves; reserve the remainder.

Bring a large saucepan of salted water to the boil and stir in the turmeric. Add the rice and simmer for 30 minutes or until the rice is just tender. Drain thoroughly and turn into a bowl.

Heat the oil in a small frying pan. Add the onion to the rice with the apricots, sultanas, spices, mint and lemon juice. Mix well together.

Take one vine leaf at a time. Place it flat on the work surface and put a heaped teaspoon of the rice mixture in the centre. Fold the base of the leaf over the filling, then fold over first one side, then the other. Fold over the top to make a neat parcel. Continue making parcels until you have used up all the filling.

Line a large frying pan with leftover vine leaves. Arrange the parcels, seam sides down, in a single layer in the pan. Cover the layer with more leaves, then make a second layer of parcels and cover them with leaves.

Pour on the orange juice and water and cover the pan. Cook gently over a low heat for 1 hour, adding a little boiling water from time to time, if necesssary.

To serve warm, allow the parcels to cool slightly in the pan, then arrange uncooked vine leaves on a flat serving dish and carefully transfer the parcels to the dish. Serve immediately.

To serve cold, allow the parcels to cool completely in the pan, then arrange on top of uncooked vine leaves on a serving dish as above. Cover and chill. *Illustrated on pages 50–1.*

SPINACH PANCAKES

15 g / ½ oz polyunsaturated margarine
500 g / 1¼ lb fresh leaf spinach, trimmed
1 small onion, peeled chopped
salt
grated nutmeg

1 × recipe Wholemeal pancakes (page 106)
40 g / 1½ oz Emmenthal cheese, grated

SERVES 4
Low Fat   High Fibre

Melt the margarine in a pan. Add the spinach, onion, salt and nutmeg to taste. Cook over a low heat for about 12 minutes then chop finely.

Make eight pancakes according to the recipe on page 106.

Spread the spinach mixture evenly over a quarter of each pancake. Fold in half and in half again to make fans. Place in a greased flameproof dish and sprinkle with the cheese. Cook under a hot grill for 3–4 minutes, until the cheese is bubbling and golden. *Illustrated on pages 68–9.*

SPINACH AND RICOTTA TRIANGLES

750 g/1½ lb spinach, trimmed, or 350 g/12 oz
  frozen spinach
350 g/12 oz Ricotta cheese
150 ml/¼ pint plain unsweetened yogurt
2 tablespoons chopped fresh chives
½ teaspoon grated nutmeg
salt and freshly ground black pepper

350 g/12 oz filo pastry
50 ml/2 fl oz vegetable oil
TO GARNISH
1 bunch watercress

MAKES 80 triangles

Filo pastry is available from delicatessens and Greek food shops. Strudel paste (page 107) may be used instead, if wished.

Cook the spinach in a very little boiling salted water for about 7 minutes, until just tender. If using frozen spinach, cook it according to packet instructions. Drain thoroughly, chop finely and leave to cool.

Combine the Ricotta with the yogurt, chives and nutmeg. Season with salt and pepper. Add the spinach and mix well.

Heat the oven to moderate (180°C, 350°F, Gas Mark 4). Place the filo pastry on a damp board and cut into 10 cm/4 inch squares, cutting through all the sheets at once. Cover with a damp cloth to keep the pastry moist while making up the triangles.

Take one square of pastry and brush with oil. Place 1 teaspoon of the spinach and cheese mixture in the middle of the square and fold over diagonally to make a triangular parcel. Continue with the pastry squares and spinach mixture until you have made about 80 triangles.

Arrange on lightly oiled baking sheets (about 10 triangles on each) and brush with oil. Bake in the oven for about 12 minutes, until nicely browned. Cool on a wire tray before serving garnished with watercress.

CONTINENTAL COURGETTES

4 small courgettes (about 350 g/12 oz),
  trimmed
salt
grated rind and juice of ½ lemon
1 hard-boiled egg, chopped
2 tablespoons cottage cheese
2 tablespoons coarsely chopped fresh mint
25 g/1 oz shelled walnuts, chopped
pinch of paprika pepper

freshly ground black pepper
TO GARNISH
lettuce leaves
lemon twists
few mint leaves

SERVES 4
Low Fat

Cook the whole courgettes in boiling, salted water for 5 minutes, then drain well. Cut in half lengthways and scoop out a channel in the centre using a teaspoon. Finely chop the scooped out flesh and set aside in a bowl.

Put the lemon rind and juice into a bowl, and add the courgette shells. Leave them to marinate in the mixture until quite cold.

Stir the chopped egg into the chopped courgette flesh with the cottage cheese, mint, walnuts, paprika pepper, salt, pepper and a little of the marinade to moisten.

Arrange two courgette shells on a bed of lettuce on each serving plate. Pile the egg mixture into the centre of the courgettes, then garnish each serving with a lemon twist and mint leaf. Serve with thinly sliced wholemeal bread.

SPINACH AND RICOTTA TRIANGLES

MARINATED MUSHROOMS

450 g/1 lb button mushrooms, trimmed and
  sliced
MARINADE
1 tablespoon cider vinegar
1 tablespoon vegetable oil
1 tablespoon lemon juice
few drops Worcestershire sauce
2 tablespoons tomato purée
2 tablespoons cold water

1 tablespoon chopped fresh mixed herbs (thyme,
  oregano, basil, tarragon), or 1½ teaspoons
  dried mixed herbs
1 small onion, peeled and grated
1 garlic clove, peeled and crushed

SERVES 4
Low Fat   Vegan

Put all the ingredients for the marinade into a large screw-top jar and shake well. Add the mushrooms, pushing them down if necessary. Shake the jar once again so the mushrooms are coated with the marinade. If you do not have a large screw-top jar, use any covered container.

Stand the jar in a cool place and leave for 24 hours, shaking occasionally so that the mushrooms soften. They will reduce in bulk considerably during this time and also produce quite an amount of liquid. Serve chilled with wholemeal rolls.

LEEKS GREEK STYLE

300 ml/½ pint water
finely grated rind and juice of 1 lemon
2 shallots, peeled and thinly sliced
4 sprigs parsley
1 small celery stick, trimmed, with leaves
1 sprig fennel or a few fennel seeds
1 sprig thyme

6 peppercorns
3 coriander seeds
salt
450 g/1 lb small leeks, trimmed

SERVES 4
Low Fat   Vegan

Put all the ingredients except the leeks, into a large pan. Bring to the boil, then lower the heat, cover and simmer for 10 minutes.

Add the leeks to the pan, cover and simmer gently for 10–15 minutes until tender but not broken up.

Transfer the leeks to a serving dish. Boil the cooking liquid until reduced by half. Strain if preferred, then pour over the leeks and leave to cool. Serve cold.

STUFFED AUBERGINES

3 large aubergines, stalks removed
1 large onion, peeled and chopped
salt
100 g/4 oz tomatoes, skinned, seeded and
  chopped
2 tablespoons chopped parsley
50 g/2 oz mushrooms, trimmed and chopped

1 teaspoon oregano
freshly ground black pepper
vegetable oil for brushing

SERVES 4
Low Fat   Vegan

Heat the oven to moderate (180°C, 350°F, Gas Mark 4).

Cut the aubergines in half lengthways. Scoop out some of the flesh and chop it finely.

Boil the onion in a very little salted water for 3–4 minutes, then drain well and add to the chopped aubergine flesh, together with the tomatoes, parsley, mushrooms, oregano and salt and pepper. Mix well and fill each aubergine half with the mixture.

Brush the top of each with oil and bake in the oven for 45 minutes–1 hour. Serve hot or cold.

GRILLED AUBERGINE

1 tablespoon wine vinegar
2 tablespoons vegetable oil
1 teaspoon sesame seed oil (optional)
salt and freshly ground black pepper
1 aubergine, about 450 g/1 lb, cut into 5 mm/¼ inch thick slices
3 teaspoons sesame seeds

SERVES 4
Vegan

Beat the vinegar, oils, salt and pepper together. Brush the aubergine slices on both sides with this mixture and put in a large fireproof dish. Allow to marinate for up to 2 hours, if possible. Place under a grill and cook until nicely brown. Turn over and coat with more of the marinade, sprinkle with sesame seeds and continue grilling until the seeds turn a golden brown. Serve with warm wholemeal pitta bread and a mixed salad.

MUSHROOMS IN GARLIC SAUCE

475 ml/16 fl oz skimmed milk
50 g/2 oz onion, peeled and chopped
½ teaspoon marjoram
½ teaspoon dried basil
salt and freshly ground black pepper
2 tablespoons wholemeal flour
4–5 cloves garlic, peeled and crushed
225 g/8 oz button mushrooms

300 ml/½ pint Vegetable stock (page 20)
100 g/4 oz Mozzarella cheese, cubed
TO GARNISH
chopped parsley

SERVES 4

Preheat the oven to moderately hot (200°C, 400°F, Gas Mark 6).

Heat 350 ml/12 fl oz of the milk, preferably in a double saucepan, with the onion, herbs and seasoning. Stir the remainder of the milk into the flour, then add a little of the hot milk. Whisk this mixture into the remainder of the hot milk in the saucepan and stir until the mixture thickens and the flour is cooked.

Wipe the mushrooms and simmer for 2 minutes in the vegetable stock. Drain the mushrooms and place in an ovenproof dish. Reserve the stock to make soup. Add the garlic to the sauce and pour over the mushrooms and sprinkle with the cheese.

Bake in the oven for 10 minutes. Finish under the grill until the top is an appetising golden brown colour.

Sprinkle with parsley before serving.

TOMATOES WITH YOGURT AND BASIL

450 g/1 lb tomatoes, skinned and coarsely
  chopped
15 g/½ oz polyunsaturated margarine
salt and freshly ground black pepper
300 ml/½ pint plain unsweetened yogurt, at
  room temperature

2 tablespoons chopped basil
25 g/1 oz pine kernels
TO GARNISH
1 flat wholemeal bread, or pitta (optional)

SERVES 4

Drain away any excess juice from the tomatoes by leaving them on a sloping board for 10 minutes.

Melt the margarine in a shallow pan and cook the tomatoes gently for a few minutes, until just softened without becoming mushy. Remove the pan from the heat. Add salt and pepper to taste.

Beat the yogurt until smooth, and stir into the tomatoes. Stir in the chopped basil, pour into a shallow serving dish and scatter the pine kernels over the top. If wished, garnish the tomatoes with triangles of flat wholemeal bread, toasted until crisp and light golden, or with pitta bread.

Serve immediately, or keep warm for a little, but do not attempt to reheat after adding the yogurt. This dish should be served warm rather than hot.

PEACHES VINAIGRETTE

4 peaches, skinned, stoned and sliced
DRESSING
good pinch of mustard powder or ¼ teaspoon
  French mustard
1 tablespoon wine vinegar
salt and freshly ground black pepper
3 tablespoons vegetable oil

1 tablespoon chopped fresh herbs (mint, parsley,
  chives, chervil, thyme, tarragon, marjoram or
  basil, or a mixture of these)

SERVES 4
Vegan

To make the dressing, mix the mustard and vinegar in a bowl and season with salt and pepper. Add the oil, a little at a time until well blended, then stir in the herbs.

Arrange the sliced peaches in a serving dish and pour over the dressing.

VARIATION
Use either one type of fruit or a mixture for this very refreshing first course. When using oranges and grapefruit, reserve the shells and use for serving instead of bowls. If using dried herbs, halve the quantity.

PINEAPPLE MADRAS

2 small pineapples, to yield about 100 g/4 oz
    flesh and 25 ml/1 fl oz of juice
1 large, ripe avocado, to yield about 200 g/7 oz
    of flesh
100 g/4 oz low fat curd cheese (e.g. quark)
½–1 teaspoon dried curry powder

50 g/2 oz seedless grapes, cut in half
TO GARNISH
4 slices orange
maraschino cherries

SERVES 4

Cut the pineapples in half lengthways, retaining some of the leaves on each of the halves. Remove the flesh, reserving the juice. If insufficient juice is extracted, make up with additional canned pineapple or orange juice as necessary. Chop the flesh finely, discarding the core. Reserve the skins.

Place the avocado flesh in a food processor or liquidizer with the cheese, curry powder and pineapple juice. Process until a thick purée has been formed. Place in a basin and fold in the pineapple and grapes.

Pile this mixture into the pineapple skins and decorate with an orange slice, threaded through a cocktail stick, topped with a maraschino cherry.

Serve on a bed of lettuce and watercress with a grilled poppadum to accompany the salad.

TABBOULEH

100 g/4 oz fine bulgar (cracked wheat)
4 spring onions, trimmed and finely chopped
4 tablespoons finely chopped fresh parsley
2 tablespoons finely chopped fresh mint
2–3 tablespoons olive oil
juice of ½ lemon

salt and freshly ground black pepper
TO GARNISH
black olives

SERVES 4
Low Fat   High Fibre   Vegan

Cover the bulgar with plenty of cold water and leave to expand for about 30 minutes. Drain the bulgar first in a sieve, then squeeze out in a piece of muslin to remove as much moisture as possible.

Mix the bulgar with the spring onions, parsley, mint, olive oil and lemon juice and season with salt and pepper.

Pile the tabbouleh into mounds on to small individual plates. Garnish each plate with black olives and serve with hot wholemeal pitta bread.

WATERCRESS WITH ORANGE AND NUTS

1 bunch watercress, trimmed
1 large orange, peeled, segmented and chopped
2 tablespoons chopped hazelnuts
DRESSING
120 ml/4 fl oz plain unsweetened yogurt
½ garlic clove, peeled and crushed with salt

2 teaspoons chopped parsley
freshly ground black pepper

SERVES 4
Low Fat

This salad is ideal for serving in individual portions in grapefruit or orange shells as an hors d'oeuvre.

Put the watercress, orange and hazelnuts into a large serving bowl.
　　To make the dressing, beat the yogurt with the garlic, parsley and pepper to taste. Pour over the watercress mixture and toss well. Leave the salad to stand for about 30 minutes before serving it to allow the flavours to develop.

GUACAMOLE

2 large very ripe avocados, halved and stoned
juice of 1 lemon
4 tomatoes, skinned, seeded and chopped
1 small onion, peeled and grated
1 garlic clove, peeled and crushed
¼ teaspoon Tabasco sauce

salt and freshly ground black pepper
1 small lettuce (optional)

SERVES 6
Vegan

If the Guacamole is not to be used immediately, reserve the avocado stones, bury them in the mixture and cover the dish – this helps to prevent the avocados from turning brown.

Scoop out the avocado pulp into a bowl and immediately pour over the lemon juice to prevent browning.
　　Mash the avocados well, then add the remaining ingredients, except the lettuce, and beat well until smooth. Alternatively, put all the ingredients in a blender and work to a smooth purée.
　　Transfer to a serving bowl, or serve on individual plates, lined with lettuce leaves. Serve the Guacamole immediately with toasted wholemeal bread.

LEBANESE PARSLEY DIP

150 ml / ¼ pint tahini
2–3 garlic cloves, peeled and crushed
150 ml / ¼ pint lemon juice
4 tablespoons water
pinch of salt
40 g / 1½ oz chopped parsley

SERVES 4–6
Vegan

Tahini is a paste made from sesame seeds and oil; it can be bought in health food shops and Eastern stores.

Beat the tahini in a bowl until smooth. Add the garlic with the lemon juice, water and salt. It should be the consistency of fairly thick cream; if necessary, thin with a little more water. Stir in the chopped parsley and serve with wholemeal pitta bread or Crudités (page 117).

Salads

TOSSED GREEN SALAD

½ lettuce, trimmed and separated into leaves
¼ bunch curly endive, trimmed
½ bunch watercress, trimmed
¼ cucumber, sliced
1 green pepper, cored, seeded and sliced

a few spring onions
120 ml/4 fl oz Vinaigrette dressing (page 40)

SERVES 4
Vegan

Put all the vegetables into a deep salad bowl. Pour over the dressing and toss well.

VARIATIONS
A basic green salad can be varied in many ways. Try adding any of the following:
APPLE WEDGES   Use red dessert apples, cored and thinly sliced.
AVOCADO SLIVERS Halve avocados, remove the stones, peel and slice the flesh. Toss in lemon juice to prevent them from turning brown.
CAULIFLOWER   SPRIGS Break   the cauliflower into small sprigs and use raw.

CHEESE   Use any kind of cheese, grated, sliced or cubed. (*Not* Vegan).
EGG   Hard-boil and thinly slice the egg before adding. (*Not* Vegan).
FRESH HERBS   Wash, dry and add, either chopped or in sprigs.
GRAPEFRUIT OR ORANGES   Cut away the peel and white pith and break the fruit into segments.
OLIVES   Drain from the jar and use whole or sliced.
NUTS   Use whole or coarsely chopped; add at the very last minute.

MIXED VEGETABLE SALAD

4 medium waxy potatoes, peeled, cooked and diced
1 large celery stalk, finely chopped
2 carrots, scrubbed and grated
1 small onion, peeled and finely chopped
½ small white cabbage, cored and shredded

2 tablespoons chopped pickled gherkins
8 black olives, stoned and chopped
3 tablespoons Vinaigrette dressing (page 40)
2 tablespoons finely chopped fresh parsley

SERVES 6

Put all the prepared ingredients in a bowl, pour over the Vinaigrette dressing, toss well, and serve.

TOP: TOSSED GREEN SALAD;
BOTTOM: WINTER SALAD (PAGE 35)

AVOCADO, GRAPEFRUIT AND SESAME SALAD

2 tablespoons sesame seeds
2 large avocados, peeled, stoned and sliced
juice of 1 lemon
2 grapefruit, peeled and segmented
1 tablespoon chopped fresh mint
lettuce leaves

SERVES 4
Vegan

Toss the sesame seeds in a dry frying pan until they begin to colour. Set aside.

Toss the avocado slices in the lemon juice to prevent discoloration. Mix in the grapefruit and mint.

Place a few lettuce leaves on four serving plates and pile the avocado mixture on top. Sprinkle over the sesame seeds and serve.

SWEETCORN AND PEPPER SALAD

1 × 300 g (11 oz) can sweetcorn niblets, drained
½ green pepper, seeded and chopped
½ red pepper, seeded and chopped
1 Spanish onion, peeled and cut into rings
4 tablespoons Vinaigrette dressing (page 40)

2 tablespoons chopped fresh parsley
1 bunch watercress, trimmed

SERVES 4
High Fibre   Vegan

Mix the sweetcorn with the green and red peppers. Reserve the larger onion rings for garnish and mix the rest into the sweetcorn mixture.

Put the dressing into a screw-top jar with the parsley and shake well, then pour over the salad ingredients.

Arrange the watercress around the outside of a salad bowl. Spoon the sweetcorn mixture into the centre and garnish with the large onion rings.

BEAN-SPROUT SALAD

225 g / 8 oz fresh or canned bean-sprouts,
    drained
1 canned pimento, drained and chopped
1 pickled cucumber, diced
1 tablespoon finely chopped fresh chives
DRESSING
2 tablespoons olive oil

1 tablespoon wine vinegar
½ teaspoon made mustard
2 teaspoons soy sauce

SERVES 4
Vegan

Put the bean-sprouts into a salad bowl with the pimento, pickled cucumber and chives.

Mix together all the ingredients for the

dressing and pour over the salad. Toss to coat thoroughly and chill for about 30 minutes before serving.

BEAN-SPROUT SALAD

COLESLAW SALAD

350 g/12 oz white cabbage, trimmed and finely
    shredded
225 g/8 oz carrots, scraped and grated
1 dessert apple, cored and chopped
25 g/1 oz sultanas
25 g/1 oz unsalted peanuts
DRESSING
1 tablespoon plain wholemeal flour
2 teaspoons French mustard

salt and freshly ground black pepper
¼ pint/150 ml wine vinegar
15 g/½ oz polyunsaturated margarine
1 egg
a little skimmed milk

SERVES 6
High Fibre

To make the dressing, put the flour and mustard into a pan. Season with salt and pepper and mix in a little vinegar to make a smooth paste, then gradually stir in the remainder. Place the pan over a low heat and, stirring all the time, bring the mixture to the boil. Simmer for 5 minutes. Remove the pan from the heat and stir in the margarine.

Beat the egg in a bowl, then gradually beat in the vinegar mixture. Return to the pan and cook until it thickens. Leave to cool, then dilute with sufficient milk to make the required consistency. Taste and adjust the seasoning.

Mix the cabbage, carrots, apple, sultanas and peanuts together in a salad bowl, then stir in enough dressing to moisten the ingredients.

TOMATO AND AVOCADO SALAD

DRESSING
4 tablespoons vegetable oil
2 tablespoons vinegar
1 teaspoon dry mustard
2 teaspoons chopped fresh marjoram
salt and freshly ground black pepper
SALAD
4 tomatoes, quartered and seeded
1 avocado, peeled, stoned and diced

100 g/4 oz fresh dates, stoned
1 × 200 g (7 oz) can red kidney beans, drained
   and rinsed
100 g/4 oz Mozzarella cheese, diced
few lettuce leaves

SERVES 4
High Fibre

Put all the dressing ingredients in a screw-top jar and shake well.

Put the tomatoes into a bowl. Add the diced avocado to the tomatoes with the dates. Mix in the beans and Mozzarella.

Pour the dressing over the salad and toss all the ingredients well together.

Line a dish with lettuce leaves, then turn the salad into the centre and chill before serving.

HOT POTATO SALAD

750 g/1½ lb new or waxy potatoes, scrubbed
2 tablespoons finely chopped onion
3 tablespoons vegetable oil
1 tablespoon white wine vinegar
salt and freshly ground black pepper
4 tablespoons chopped chives

SERVES 4
Vegan

Cook the potatoes in their skins in boiling, salted water for about 20 minutes until tender. Drain well and cut into thick slices. Stir in the chopped onion. Pour over the oil and vinegar, and mix gently, trying not to break the potatoes. Season with salt and pepper and stir in 3 tablespoons of the chives.

Turn the salad into a serving dish and scatter the remaining chives over the top.

RED CABBAGE SALAD

450 g/1 lb red cabbage, trimmed and finely
   shredded
225 g/8 oz carrots, scraped and grated
50 g/2 oz raisins
2 large oranges, rinds grated, flesh divided into
   segments

2 tablespoons mayonnaise
2 tablespoons plain unsweetened yogurt

SERVES 4
High Fibre

Put the cabbage into a bowl with the carrots and raisins, and add the orange segments.

Mix the mayonnaise and yogurt together and stir in the orange rind.

Just before serving, mix the dressing into the salad and toss well.

WINTER SALAD

1 tablespoon sesame seeds
1 carrot, scraped and finely grated
75 g/3 oz raw mushrooms, wiped and finely
    sliced
50 g/2 oz cooked beetroot, peeled and cubed
¼ small onion, finely chopped

1 large sprig parsley, finely chopped
¼ bunch watercress, chopped
1–2 tablespoons balsamic vinegar (page 41)

SERVES 4
Low Fat   Vegan

Toss the sesame seeds in a thick frying pan over a moderate heat until a light golden colour. Cool on absorbent kitchen paper.

Then mix in a salad bowl with all the other ingredients and serve.

BROWN RICE SALAD

225 g/8 oz brown rice
12 whole cardamom seeds
salt
1 × 200 g (7 oz) can pineapple rings, drained
    and roughly chopped
½ cucumber, diced
50 g/2 oz hazelnuts, roasted

DRESSING
grated rind and juice of 1 orange
3 tablespoons vegetable oil
2 teaspoons curry paste

SERVES 4
High Fibre   Vegan

Cook the rice with the cardamom seeds in boiling salted water for 40 minutes or until the rice is just tender. Drain the rice and run cold water through the grains to remove any excess starch.

Mix the chopped pineapple into the rice with the cucumber and hazelnuts.

Put all the dressing ingredients in a screw-top jar and shake well. Stir the dressing through the rice salad so that it is evenly coated.

CHICORY AND FRUIT SALAD

5 heads chicory, trimmed and thinly sliced into
    rings
2 celery hearts, trimmed and thinly sliced into
    rings
4 oranges, peeled and segmented
225 g/8 oz seedless white grapes
225 g/8 oz black grapes, halved and seeded
2 bunches watercress, trimmed
100 g/4 oz button mushrooms, thinly sliced

DRESSING
4 tablespoons vegetable oil
1 tablespoon orange juice
2 teaspoons lemon juice
2 spring onions, trimmed and thinly sliced
salt and freshly ground black pepper

SERVES 4
Vegan

Toss together the chicory, celery, oranges, grapes, watercress and mushrooms.

Mix together all the ingredients for the dressing, with salt and pepper to taste.

About 1 hour before serving, pour the dressing on to the salad and toss to mix well.

CUCUMBER AND TOMATO RAITA

1 small or ½ large cucumber, sliced
4 tomatoes, thinly sliced
300 ml / ½ pint plain unsweetened yogurt
2 tablespoons chopped mint
freshly ground white pepper
TO GARNISH
mint sprig

SERVES 4
Low Fat

Arrange the cucumber and tomatoes in a serving dish. Mix the yogurt with the chopped mint and pepper to taste, then pour over the salad. Garnish with mint. Serve chilled.

ITALIAN SALAD

½ head curly endive, trimmed and separated
*   into leaves*
1 head chicory, trimmed and sliced into rings
1 bulb fennel, trimmed and sliced into rings
1 small head radiccio, trimmed and separated
*   into leaves (optional)*
8 radishes, trimmed and sliced if large
4 tablespoons Vinaigrette dressing (page 40)
salt and freshly ground black pepper

SERVES 4
Low Fat

Put all the ingredients into a salad bowl, toss well, then taste and adjust the seasoning. Serve cold.

LEFT: CUCUMBER AND TOMATO RAITA;
RIGHT: ITALIAN SALAD

TOMATO AND FENNEL SALAD

2 bunches spring onions, trimmed and thinly
    sliced
½ small Florence fennel (about 100 g/4 oz)
    trimmed and thinly sliced horizontally
350 g/12 oz tomatoes, skinned and chopped
25 g/1 oz parsley, coarsely chopped

5 tablespoons coarsely chopped mint
2 tablespoons vegetable oil
1 tablespoon lemon juice

SERVES 4
Vegan

Put the spring onions into a bowl with the fennel and the tomatoes. Mix in the parsley and mint. Pour over the oil and lemon juice and mix again.

RED APPLE AND SAMPHIRE SALAD

100 g/4 oz samphire
½ small head celery, finely chopped
1 bunch watercress, finely chopped
3 red dessert apples, cored and sliced
DRESSING
1 tablespoon plain unsweetened yogurt
1 tablespoon mayonnaise

SERVES 4

Samphire grows on cliffs and can be bought from enterprising fishmongers. If unobtainable, substitute bean-shoots.

Remove any discoloured pieces of the samphire, chop roughly. Rinse well in cold water. Plunge into boiling water. Allow the water to come to the boil, simmer for 1 minute and drain. Rinse in cold water and set aside to cool.

Assemble all the ingredients in a large salad bowl and toss with the salad dressing.

APPLE AND CELERIAC SALAD

750 g/1½ lb celeriac
3 tablespoons plain unsweetened yogurt
2 tablespoons mayonnaise
1 tablespoon finely chopped chervil or borage
1 tablespoon finely chopped fresh parsley
2 crisp red dessert apples, cored and thinly sliced
    into rings
100 g/4 oz cashew nuts, finely chopped

SERVES 6
High Fibre

Put the celeriac into a saucepan and cover with water. Bring to the boil, lower the heat and cook for 15 minutes. Drain thoroughly, allow to cool, then peel and cube.

Mix together the yogurt, mayonnaise, chervil or borage and parsley. Add the apple slices to the yogurt mixture with the celeriac. Stir to coat and transfer to a salad bowl. Sprinkle the nuts over and serve.

WHITE BEAN SALAD

*225 g / 8 oz dried white beans (haricot, butter
 and black-eye peas), soaked overnight in cold
 water*
600 ml / 1 pint water
1 onion, peeled and chopped
1 bay leaf
2 hard-boiled eggs, cut into wedges
8 black olives
DRESSING
3 tablespoons vegetable oil

grated rind and juice of 1 small lemon
1 tablespoon capers
2 gherkins, sliced
2 tablespoons chopped fresh parsley
salt and freshly ground black pepper

SERVES 4
High Fibre

Drain the beans, reserve the liquid and make up to 600 ml / 1 pint with water. Place the beans and water in a saucepan and add the onion and bay leaf. Cover and bring to the boil. Simmer for 45 minutes–1 hour until the beans are tender. Drain and leave to cool thoroughly.

To make the dressing, mix together the ingredients and season to taste. Pour half the dressing over the beans and leave to marinate for at least 30 minutes.

Turn the beans into a serving dish and arrange the eggs and olives on the top. Add the remaining dressing and serve.

GARLIC AND HERB SAUCE

150 ml / ¼ pint plain unsweetened yogurt
1 large garlic clove, crushed with a pinch of salt
salt and freshly ground black pepper
*2 tablespoons chopped mixed herbs (parsley,
 chives, dill and tarragon)*

SERVES 4
Low Fat

Gradually beat the yogurt into the crushed garlic, pounding all the time. When it has all been added, season with salt and black

pepper. Stir in the chopped herbs and chill until ready to serve. Serve this sauce with Stuffed aubergines (pages 24–5).

WATERCRESS MAYONNAISE

1½ tablespoons cornflour
1 teaspoon celery seed
1 teaspoon dried mustard
1 teaspoon salt
freshly ground black pepper
250 ml / 8 fl oz skimmed milk

2 egg yolks, beaten
50 ml / 2 fl oz vinegar
1 bunch watercress, washed

MAKES 300 ml / ½ pint
Low Fat

Mix together the cornflour, celery seed, mustard and salt in a small heavy-based saucepan. Beat in the milk a little at a time and cook over a low heat, stirring constantly, until the mixture thickens. Continue to cook for 2 minutes. Cool slightly,

add the beaten egg yolks and cook for a further 2–3 minutes. Remove from the heat and stir in the vinegar. Place in a liquidizer or food processor with the watercress and blend. Chill before serving. The mayonnaise may be refrigerated for 2–3 days.

VINAIGRETTE DRESSING

*1 tablespoon wine vinegar or balsamic vinegar
(page 41)*
1 tablespoon water
2 tablespoons olive, walnut or corn oil
salt and freshly ground black pepper

SERVES 4
Vegan

Place the ingredients in a screw-top jar or
bottle and shake thoroughly to mix. Shake
again before serving.

MUSTARD AND DILL DRESSING

1½ teaspoons Dijon mustard
1½ teaspoons vegetable oil
4 tablespoons plain unsweetened yogurt
juice of ½ lemon
2 tablespoons chopped dill

MAKES sufficient to dress 1 salad

Put the mustard into a bowl and stir in the
oil drop by drop, as if making mayonnaise.
When the mustard and oil have blended
together smoothly, stir in the yogurt. Add
lemon juice to taste and stir in the chopped
dill.

If at any stage the sauce separates, purée
it in a blender to emulsify.

COS LETTUCE WITH YOGURT DRESSING

1 cos lettuce, trimmed, leaves torn
3–4 tablespoons plain unsweetened yogurt
1 garlic clove, peeled and crushed
1 teaspoon tomato purée
salt and freshly ground white pepper

SERVES 4
Low Fat

Put the lettuce leaves into a salad bowl.
   To make the dressing, mix the yogurt with the garlic, tomato purée, and salt and pepper to taste, until smooth.
   Pour the dressing over the lettuce and toss thoroughly to coat. Serve at once.

MUSHROOM SALAD WITH HERBS

225 g/8 oz very fresh button mushrooms, stalks
   removed, caps thinly sliced
salt and freshly ground black pepper
2 tablespoons finely chopped onion
1 garlic clove, peeled and crushed
3 tablespoons vegetable oil

1½ tablespoons lemon juice
2 tablespoons chopped chervil
2 tablespoons chopped chives

SERVES 4
Vegan

Put the mushroom caps into a serving bowl and season with salt and pepper. Stir in the onion and garlic. Stir in the oil, lemon juice and chopped herbs. Serve soon after making, or the mushrooms will dry up and need yet more oil.

TOMATO AND MOZZARELLA SALAD WITH BASIL

450 g/1 lb tomatoes, skinned and thinly sliced
225 g/8 oz Mozzarella cheese, thinly sliced
salt and freshly ground black pepper
3–4 teaspoons balsamic vinegar
1½ tablespoons chopped basil

SERVES 4

Balsamic vinegar is a centuries-old speciality from Modena and is produced from sauvignon and lambrusco grapes aged for years in mulberry, chestnut and juniper wood vats. This results in such a mellow vinegar that it can flavour salads without the addition of oil. It is obtainable from speciality delicatessens.

Lay the sliced tomatoes on one half of a flat serving dish and the cheese on the other half. Season the tomatoes with salt and black pepper, the Mozzarella with pepper only. Pour over the vinegar and scatter the chopped basil over all. Allow the salad to stand for a little time before serving.

TOMATO AND MOZZARELLA SALAD WITH BASIL

Main Course Dishes

DEEP DISH VEGETABLE PIE

15 g / ½ oz polyunsaturated margarine
1 teaspoon cumin seeds, crushed
1 teaspoon coriander seeds, crushed
450 g / 1 lb small carrots, scraped and quartered
   lengthways
225 g / 8 oz small potatoes, scraped and diced
1 medium cauliflower, trimmed and cut into
   florets
225 g / 8 oz small white turnips, peeled and
   diced
225 g / 8 oz courgettes, trimmed and sliced
225 g / 8 oz shelled broad beans
225 g / 8 oz young French beans, trimmed
300 ml / ½ pint water
SAUCE
40 g / 1½ oz polyunsaturated margarine

1 medium onion, peeled and chopped
2 garlic cloves, peeled and crushed
1 tablespoon medium curry powder
1½ tablespoons plain wholemeal flour
300 ml / ½ pint skimmed milk
salt and freshly ground black pepper
2 tablespoons chopped fresh parsley
PASTRY
1 recipe Wholemeal shortcrust pastry (page
   106)
TO GLAZE
beaten egg

SERVES 4
High Fibre

Heat the margarine in a large pan and fry the cumin seeds until they begin to pop. Add the vegetables and fry until lightly browned. Stir in the water and bring to the boil, then cover and simmer until the vegetables are just tender. Drain the vegetables, reserving the liquid.

To make the sauce, melt the margarine in a saucepan, add the onion and garlic and fry over a moderate heat for 3 minutes, stirring occasionally. Stir in the curry powder and cook for 1 minute. Stir in the flour and cook for a further 1 minute. Add 120 ml (4 fl oz) of the vegetable cooking water and stir. Add the milk and stir until the sauce thickens. Season to taste with salt and pepper. Stir the vegetables and parsley into the sauce and mix well.

Place a pie funnel in the centre of a 2 litre (3½ pint) deep pie dish. Spoon the vegetables and sauce into the dish and leave to cool. Heat the oven to 200°C, 400°F, Gas Mark 6.

Roll out the pastry on a lightly floured board. Cut a strip of dough to fit the rim of the dish. Dampen the rim and press on the pastry strip. Cover the dish with the remaining dough and press to the strip on the rim. Trim the edges and flute them. Brush the pastry with beaten egg. Re-roll the pastry trimmings and cut out leaf shapes. Arrange them on the pie and brush them with beaten egg. Stand the dish on a baking sheet. Bake in the oven for 20–25 minutes or until the top is golden brown.

VEGETABLE PIE WITH HERB PASTRY

25 g/1 oz polyunsaturated margarine
175 g/6 oz onions, peeled and sliced
175 g/6 oz carrots, scraped and chopped
225 g/8 oz new potatoes, scrubbed and sliced
225 g/8 oz broad beans, shelled
225 g/8 oz fresh peas, shelled
100 g/4 oz mushrooms, sliced
225 g/8 oz tomatoes, sliced
1 teaspoon yeast extract
just under 300 ml/½ pint tepid water

HERB PASTRY
225 g/8 oz plain wholemeal flour
2 teaspoons baking powder
pinch of salt
100 g/4 oz polyunsaturated margarine
2 teaspoons dried mixed herbs
cold water

SERVES 4
High Fibre

Melt the margarine in a saucepan, add the onions, carrots and potatoes and gently fry for about 7 minutes, then turn into a large pie dish. Place the beans, peas and mushrooms on top, then arrange the slices of tomato on top. Leave the pie dish on one side.

To make the pastry, sift the flour, baking powder and salt together into a mixing bowl, add the margarine and rub in until evenly distributed. Mix in the herbs, then bind the ingredients together with enough cold water to make a soft but not sticky dough. Knead the dough lightly until smooth. Heat the oven to moderately hot (190°C, 375°F, Gas Mark 5).

Dissolve the yeast extract in the water and pour sufficient into the dish to come within 2.5 cm (1 inch) of the rim. Roll out the pastry and cover the pie, leave in a cool place for 15 minutes. Cook in the oven for 30 minutes, then reduce the temperature to 160°C, 325°F, Gas Mark 3, and cook for a further 30 minutes until the pastry is cooked.

VEGETABLE LOAF

100 g/4 oz mushrooms, trimmed
4 stuffed green olives, sliced
25 g/1 oz polyunsaturated margarine
1 large onion, peeled and chopped
100 g/4 oz brown rice, cooked
100 g/4 oz peas, cooked
1 tablespoon tomato purée
1 tablespoon soy sauce

½ teaspoon ground allspice
2 eggs, beaten
2 hard-boiled eggs
TO GARNISH
sliced tomatoes

SERVES 4
High Fibre

Heat the oven to hot (220°C, 425°F, Gas Mark 7) and grease a 450 g (1 lb) loaf tin. Line the base with greaseproof paper and brush it with oil.

Thinly slice two of the mushrooms and arrange them in a line down the centre of the tin and place a row of sliced stuffed olives on either side.

Melt the margarine in a saucepan. Chop the rest of the mushrooms and add to the pan with the onion, then fry gently until beginning to soften. Remove from the heat and stir in the rice, peas, tomato purée, soy sauce, allspice and beaten eggs.

Spoon half the mixture into the loaf tin. Arrange the hard-boiled eggs lengthways in the tin and spoon the rest of the mixture on top, pressing it well down.

Put a piece of greased greaseproof paper on top of the mixture and cook in the oven for 35–40 minutes or until firm to the touch. Leave to cool in the tin, then carefully turn it on to a serving plate and garnish with lettuce and tomatoes.

VEGETABLE STRUDEL

50 g/2 oz brown lentils
350 ml/12 fl oz water
50 g/2 oz onions, peeled and chopped
1 teaspoon oil
¼ teaspoon ground cumin
¼ teaspoon grond ginger
1 garlic clove, peeled and crushed
75 g/3 oz mushrooms, wiped and sliced
1 tablespoon fresh chopped herbs (parsley,
    thyme, basil, tarragon, chives)

100 g/4 oz tomatoes, peeled
150 ml/5 fl oz Vegetable stock (page 20)
2 teaspoons tomato paste
salt and freshly ground black pepper
75 g/3 oz filo pastry
2 teaspoons vegetable oil

SERVES 4
Low Fat   High Fibre

Place the lentils in a pan, cover with the water, bring to the boil and simmer for about one hour or until they are soft but not mushy. Meanwhile, cook the onions in the oil in a non-stick pan until soft and transparent. Add the cumin, ginger, garlic, mushrooms and herbs. Cook a further two minutes.

Add the tomatoes, stock, tomato paste and seasoning. Once the tomatoes have softened add the lentils and continue cooking until the mixture resembles a soft paste. Set aside to cool. Cut the filo pastry into three 36 cm/14 inch squares. Brush each pastry square lightly with oil and place one on top of the other.

Spread the cooked vegetable filling over the pastry, leaving a 2.5 cm/1 inch border around the edge. Brush this border with cold water. Fold the pastry in half and press the edges together to seal. Brush the pastry with a little oil.

Carefully place on a lightly greased baking tray. Make several slits along the top of the strudel. Bake in a moderately hot oven (180°C, 350°F, Gas Mark 4) for 15 to 25 minutes, until lightly brown.

Cut into slices and serve with a crisp green salad.

PASTA WITH RATATOUILLE SAUCE

1 large onion, peeled and chopped
1 garlic clove, peeled and crushed
450 g/1 lb courgettes, trimmed and sliced
1 large aubergine, stalk removed, diced
1 green pepper, cored, seeded and diced
450 g/1 lb tomatoes, skinned and chopped
1 tablespoon chopped oregano or basil
salt and freshly ground black pepper

450 g/1 lb wholemeal pasta (spaghetti or
    noodles)
TO GARNISH
1 tablespoon chopped parsley
grated Parmesan cheese

SERVES 4–6
Low Fat   High Fibre

Put all the ingredients, except the pasta, into a large pan. Cover and cook gently for 30 minutes until the vegetables are tender and the juices have thickened slightly, stirring occasionally.

Meanwhile, cook the pasta in a large pan with plenty of boiling, salted water until just tender (about 5 minutes for freshly made pasta and 15 minutes for dried). Drain and pile into a warmed serving dish.

Taste and adjust the seasoning of the sauce, then pour over the pasta. Sprinkle with the parsley and grated Parmesan cheese. Serve hot.

LEFT: PASTA WITH RATATOUILLE SAUCE;
RIGHT: BROCCOLI PANCAKES

BROCCOLI PANCAKES

8 Wholemeal pancakes (page 106), kept warm
FILLING
450 g / 1 lb broccoli spears, trimmed
25 g / 1 oz polyunsaturated margarine
25 g / 1 oz wholemeal flour
300 ml / ½ pint skimmed milk

100 g / 4 oz Gruyère or Cheddar cheese, grated
freshly ground black pepper

MAKES 8 pancakes
High Fibre

Heat the oven to moderately hot (200°C, 400°F, Gas Mark 6).

To make the filling, cook the broccoli in boiling water for 5–10 minutes until tender, then drain thoroughly and keep warm.

Melt the margarine in a pan. Add the flour and cook for 1–2 minutes, stirring constantly. Remove from the heat and gradually stir in the milk. Return to the heat and simmer until the sauce is thick and smooth, stirring constantly. Stir in the cheese, reserving a little for the topping,

then add pepper to taste.

Divide the broccoli equally between the pancakes, then roll up and place in an ovenproof dish. Pour over the sauce and sprinkle with the reserved cheese.

Bake in the oven for 10–15 minutes until heated through. Serve hot.

Alternatively, leave the pancakes until cold before filling, then cover and bake for 15 minutes. Uncover and bake for a further 10–15 minutes until hot and bubbling. Serve hot.

BEAN AND CHEESE PANCAKES

8 Wholemeal pancakes (page 106)
FILLING
25 g/8 oz cottage cheese
2 × 225 g (8 oz) cans curried beans with
    sultanas

TOPPING
150 ml/¼ pint skimmed milk soft cheese
chopped chives

SERVES 4
Low Fat　High Fibre

Grease a large shallow ovenproof dish and heat the oven to moderately hot (190°C, 375°F, Gas Mark 5).

For the filling, mix the cottage cheese and the curried beans and season with salt and pepper. Divide the filling between the pancakes and roll up each one. Arrange in the dish, cover with foil and cook in the oven for about 8 minutes.

Meanwhile, heat the soft cheese over a low heat, spoon over the heated pancakes and serve sprinkled with chopped chives.

GREEK RICE RING

2 tablespoons vegetable oil
1 onion, peeled and sliced
1 garlic clove, peeled and crushed
225 g/8 oz brown rice
750 ml/1¼ pints water
salt
1 green pepper, cored, seeded and chopped
50 g/2 oz dried apricots, soaked and sliced

50 g/2 oz dried prunes, soaked, stoned and
    sliced
75 g/3 oz shelled walnuts, roughly chopped
50 g/2 oz black olives, halved and stoned
freshly ground black pepper

SERVES 4
High Fibre　　Vegan

Fill the centre of this rice ring with a crisp green salad or vegetables of your choice such as Courgettes Provençales (page 67).

Heat the oil in a large pan and gently fry the onion and garlic until soft. Stir in the rice and cook, stirring for 1 minute. Add the water and season with salt. Bring to the boil, cover and simmer for 20 minutes.

Heat the oven to moderate (180°C, 350°F, Gas Mark 4).

Stir the green pepper, apricots and prunes into the rice mixture. Continue to simmer, covered, for about 20 minutes or until the rice is cooked and the liquid absorbed. Stir in the walnuts, olives and salt and pepper to taste.

Turn the mixture into a greased 900 ml/ (1½ pint) ring mould and cook in the oven for 30 minutes. Turn out. Serve hot or cold.

WHOLEMEAL LASAGNE

225 g/8 oz wholemeal lasagne
few drops of vegetable oil
600 ml/1 pint Fresh tomato sauce (page 52)
225 g/8 oz Ricotta, curd or sieved cottage cheese
50 g/2 oz Parmesan cheese
WHITE SAUCE
25 g/1 oz polyunsaturated margarine

2 tablespoons plain wholemeal flour
150 ml/¼ pint hot skimmed milk
salt and freshly ground black pepper
pinch of grated nutmeg

SERVES 6
Low Fat　High Fibre

Cook the lasagne in boiling water, to which a few drops of oil have been added, for 10–20 minutes or until just tender. Drain on a clean teatowel.

Heat the oven to moderate (180°C, 350°F, Gas Mark 4).

Spread one-quarter of the Fresh tomato sauce over the bottom of a greased deep ovenproof dish. Cover with one-third of the lasagne, then one-third of the soft cheese. Sprinkle with 1 teaspoon of the Parmesan cheese. Repeat the layers twice, then spoon over the remaining sauce.

To make the white sauce, melt the margarine in a pan, stir in the flour and cook for 2 minutes. Gradually stir in the milk and simmer until thickened. Season with salt, pepper and nutmeg then pour over the lasagne.

Sprinkle over the remaining Parmesan cheese. Cook in the oven for 30–35 minutes until lightly browned and hot.

TAGLIATELLE WITH FRESH TOMATO AND BASIL SAUCE

225 g/8 oz wholemeal tagliatelle
salt
SAUCE
1 tablespoon vegetable oil
1 onion, peeled and thinly sliced
1 garlic clove, peeled and crushed
450–750 g/1–1½ lb tomatoes, peeled and cut into wedges

1 tablespoon fresh basil, chopped (or mint and parsley)
freshly ground black pepper

SERVES 4
Low Fat   Vegan

Cook the tagliatelle in a large pan of boiling salted water for 15–20 minutes (depending on whether the pasta is fresh or dried) until it is just tender.

Meanwhile, make the sauce, heat the oil in a non-stick saucepan and fry the onion and garlic for 5 minutes until lightly browned. Add the tomatoes and cook, stirring occasionally, for a further 5 minutes, to make a thick sauce with pieces of whole tomato.

Drain the pasta and place in a serving dish. Pour over the tomato sauce and serve.

LENTILS IN TOMATO SAUCE

225 g/8 oz brown or green lentils
1 × 400g (14 oz) can tomatoes, chopped
600 ml/1 pint water
1 onion, peeled and chopped
1 tablespoon chopped fresh oregano, marjoram or basil, or 1 teaspoon dried herbs
salt and freshly ground black pepper

SERVES 4
Low Fat   High Fibre   Vegan

Serve this dish hot or cold, sprinkled with chopped marjoram or parsley, as a vegetable accompaniment.

Put the lentils into a saucepan. Add the tomatoes with their juice. Pour over the water and add the onion and herbs. Season with salt and pepper, cover the pan and bring to the boil.

Simmer gently for 1–1¼ hours until the lentils are tender and most of the liquid has evaporated, but the mixture is still moist. Stir occasionally towards the end of cooking to prevent the lentils sticking.

PIZZA WITH DRIED HERBS

DOUGH
1 teaspoon dried yeast
150 ml / ¼ pint tepid water
pinch of sugar
225 g / 8 oz strong wholemeal flour
½ teaspoon salt
TOPPING
300 ml / ½ pint Thick tomato sauce (page 52)

1 teaspoon dried oregano
½ teaspoon dried thyme
75–100 g / 3–4 oz Mozzarella cheese, coarsely grated
1 tablespoon freshly grated Parmesan cheese

SERVES 4
High Fibre

To make the dough, put the yeast in a cup with 2 tablespoons of the warm water, and a pinch of sugar. Leave in a warm place for 10 minutes until frothy.

Sift the flour with the salt into a large bowl. Stir in the bran remaining in the sieve. Make a depression in the centre of the flour and pour in the yeast liquid and the remaining warm water. Beat with a wooden spoon until it all clings together, adding more water if required, then turn out on to a floured surface and knead for 5 minutes.

Put the dough back into a clean bowl, lightly oiled, and cover it with cling film. Stand the bowl in a warm place for 1–2 hours until the dough has roughly doubled in volume. When the dough has risen sufficiently, knock it back and turn out on to a floured board. Knead again briefly for 2–3 minutes and divide into two.

Heat the oven to hot (220°C, 425°F, Gas Mark 7).

Roll each piece of dough out fairly thinly. Pick up each one and pull it gently between the hands to make a large thin round, roughly 25 cm (10 inches) across. Lay the two circles of dough on oiled baking sheets and cover each one with 150 ml / ¼ pint of the Thick tomato sauce, spreading it evenly almost up to the edge. Sprinkle over each one ½ teaspoon dried oregano and ¼ teaspoon dried thyme. Scatter half the Mozzarella over each pizza and sprinkle the grated Parmesan on top. Bake for about 12 minutes in the oven or until the edges of the dough are browned and the centre lightly coloured.

CHEESE SOUFFLÉ

15 g / ½ oz polyunsaturated margarine
25 g / 1 oz plain flour
300 ml / ½ pint skimmed milk
2 egg yolks
75 g / 3 oz Cheddar cheese, grated

salt and freshly ground black pepper
grated nutmeg
4 egg whites

SERVES 3

Grease a 1.2 litre (2 pint) soufflé dish and heat the oven to moderately hot (190°C, 375°F, Gas Mark 5).

Melt the margarine in a saucepan, stir in the flour and cook for 1 minute. Remove from the heat and gradually blend in the milk. Cook, stirring, until the sauce thickens. Simmer, stirring, for 2 minutes, then remove from the heat and cool slightly. Beat in the egg yolks and cheese and season with salt, pepper and nutmeg.

Whisk the egg whites until stiff and fold into the cheese mixture quickly. Turn into the soufflé dish and cook in the oven for 30–35 minutes until well risen and golden brown. Serve immediately.

CHEESE SOUFFLÉ

SPINACH SOUFFLÉ

15 g/½ oz polyunsaturated margarine
1 garlic clove, peeled
1 small onion, peeled and finely chopped
400 g/14 oz fresh leaf spinach, trimmed and
 finely chopped
salt
grated nutmeg

3 eggs, separated
2 tablespoons skimmed milk
1 tablespoon grated Parmesan cheese
1 teaspoon lemon juice

SERVES 4
High Fibre

Grease a 1.2 litre (2 pint) soufflé dish. Heat the oven to moderately hot (200°C, 400°F, Gas Mark 6).

Melt the margarine in a flameproof casserole, add the garlic and fry until golden brown. Remove the garlic with a slotted spoon. Add the onion to the casserole and cook until softened. Add the spinach and season with salt and nutmeg to taste.

Cook for 2–3 minutes, then remove from the heat.

Beat the egg yolks with the milk and stir into the spinach mixture with the cheese. Whisk the egg whites and lemon juice until stiff, then fold into the spinach mixture with a metal spoon.

Spoon into the soufflé dish and cook in the oven for about 30 minutes until golden, well risen and just firm to the touch. Serve immediately.

BUTTER BEAN, HERB AND TOMATO SOUFFLÉ

*100 g / 4 oz butter beans, soaked overnight in
  cold water*
600 ml / 1 pint water
150 ml / ¼ pint skimmed milk
1 large onion, peeled and grated
4 tomatoes, skinned and chopped
1 tablespoon chopped parsley
1 tablespoon chopped thyme
1 teaspoon chopped sage
salt and freshly ground white pepper
4 eggs, separated

SERVES 4
Low Fat   High Fibre

Transfer the beans and water to a pan then bring to the boil. Lower the heat, cover and simmer for about 1½ hours until the beans are soft, adding water if needed.

Heat the oven to moderate (180°C, 350°F, Gas Mark 4).

Drain the beans, return to the rinsed-out pan and mash well. Add the milk and onion and bring to the boil, stirring constantly. Simmer for 1 minute. Remove the pan from the heat, then stir in the tomatoes and herbs. Season with salt and pepper and stir in the egg yolks and leave to cool slightly.

Beat the egg whites until just stiff, then fold into the bean sauce. Pour the mixture into a 1.5 litre (2½ pint) soufflé dish. Bake in the oven for 1 hour until the soufflé has risen and is lightly browned on top. Serve immediately.

PISTOU

1 large ripe tomato, cut in half horizontally
40 g / 1½ oz chopped basil
4 tablespoons pine kernels, chopped
2 garlic cloves, peeled and crushed
25 g / 1 oz Parmesan cheese, freshly grated
50 ml / 2 fl oz vegetable oil

MAKES about 150 ml / ¼ pint

This sauce should have the consistency of creamed butter. Serve with wholemeal spaghetti, tagliatelle, gnocchi, noodles, or in a minestrone-type soup.

Grill the tomato until soft and quite blackened on the surface. Remove the skin and chop the flesh. Put the chopped basil in a mortar and pound until crushed. Add the pine kernels and garlic and pound again. Add the chopped tomato and continue to pound, finally adding the grated cheese. When smooth, pour on the oil drop by drop, as if making mayonnaise, continuing to pound constantly.

LEFT: SPINACH SOUFFLÉ; RIGHT: VINE-LEAF PARCELS (PAGES 20–1)

FRESH TOMATO SAUCE

1 kg/2 lb ripe tomatoes, chopped
1 onion, peeled and finely chopped
1 carrot, scraped and finely chopped
1 celery stick, trimmed and finely chopped
1 small leek, trimmed and chopped
½ teaspoon salt
½ teaspoon dried oregano

½ teaspoon dried basil
1 tablespoon tomato purée
freshly ground black pepper

MAKES about 600 ml/1 pint
Low Fat   Vegan

It is worth making the full amount when tomatoes are plentiful, and freezing or refrigerating any surplus.

Put all the ingredients into a saucepan and bring to the boil. Stir, then cover tightly and simmer for 40–45 minutes.

Purée in a liquidizer or food processor and strain into a clean pan.

Boil, uncovered, for a few minutes to thicken the sauce, then taste and adjust the seasoning.

THICK TOMATO SAUCE

1 tablespoon vegetable oil
1 medium onion, peeled and chopped
1 garlic clove, peeled and crushed
1½ × 400 g (14 oz) cans Italian plum tomatoes
4 tablespoons tomato purée
salt and freshly ground black pepper

½ bay leaf
2 teaspoons chopped basil

MAKES about 450 ml/¾ pint
Low Fat   Vegan

Heat the oil in a broad pan. Cook the onion slowly until softened. Do not let the onion colour more than a pale yellow. Add the garlic towards the end. Pour in the canned tomatoes with their juice and the tomato purée. Chop roughly in the pan with the edge of a palette knife. Add the salt, pepper and bay leaf. Simmer slowly for 1 hour with the lid off, until reduced to a thick sauce, stirring now and then. Add the chopped basil for the last few minutes only.

LENTIL PATTIES

1 tablespoon vegetable oil
1 garlic clove, peeled and crushed
1 onion, peeled and finely chopped
1 celery stick, trimmed and chopped
1 carrot, scraped and chopped
225 g/8 oz brown lentils
900 ml/1½ pints water
salt and freshly ground black pepper
4 tablespoons wholemeal flour

½ teaspoon ground ginger
½ teaspoon ground cumin
1 teaspoon curry powder
1 tablespoon mango chutney, chopped
1 teaspoon vegetable oil for shallow frying

SERVES 6
Low Fat   High Fibre   Vegan

Heat the oil in a large saucepan and gently fry the garlic, onion, celery and carrot until they begin to soften.

Add the lentils and water and season with salt and pepper. Bring to the boil, then lower the heat, cover and simmer gently for about 1 hour until the lentils are soft and all the liquid is absorbed.

Add 2 tablespoons of the flour, the spices and chutney to the pan and mix well. Continue to cook gently for 2–3 minutes, stirring constantly. Adjust the seasoning if necessary. Turn the mixture on to a plate and leave until cool enough to handle.

Divide the mixture into 18 equal pieces and form each into a patty, about 1 cm (½ inch) thick. Coat with the remaining flour. Heat a little oil in a non-stick frying pan and fry the lentil patties, a few at a time, until crisp and golden brown, turning once.

Serve the patties on a bed of brown rice, topped with Fresh tomato sauce (opposite).

SPANISH VEGETABLE OMELETTE

2 tablespoons vegetable oil
4 large boiled potatoes, chopped or sliced
2 onions, peeled and chopped
1 red pepper, cored, seeded and chopped or cut
    into strips
1 green pepper, cored, seeded and chopped or cut
    into strips
2 courgettes, cut into julienne strips

2 small aubergines, finely chopped
2–3 cloves garlic, peeled and crushed
350 g/12 oz tomatoes, finely chopped
3 eggs
salt

SERVES 4

Heat the oil in a large non-stick pan, add the potatoes and fry, over a low heat, turning frequently, for about 5 minutes.

Add the onions, peppers, courgettes and aubergines and fry, over a low heat, for about 8–10 minutes. Just before the vegetables are cooked, add the garlic and finely chopped tomatoes.

Beat the eggs with a little salt. Pour the mixture evenly over the vegetables and cook, over a low heat, until the egg has just set.

Turn the omelette out on to a large plate and serve cut into wedges.

BRAZIL MUSHROOM CASSEROLE

450 g/1 lb small button mushrooms, trimmed
4 tomatoes, sliced
4 spring onions, trimmed and chopped
1 tablespoon chopped oregano or marjoram
1 tablespoon chopped basil
1 teaspoon chopped rosemary leaves
salt and freshly ground black pepper

4 tablespoons dry white wine or Vegetable stock
    (page 20)
100 g/4 oz shelled Brazil nuts, coarsely ground
50 g/2 oz fresh wholemeal breadcrumbs

SERVES 4
Low Fat   High Fibre   Vegan

Heat the oven to moderately hot (190°C, 375°F, Gas Mark 5).

Arrange the mushrooms, tomatoes and spring onions in layers in an ovenproof dish, sprinkling each layer with the herbs and salt and pepper to taste. Pour on the wine or stock. Mix the nuts and breadcrumbs together and sprinkle over the top of the dish. Bake in the oven for 20–30 minutes until the mushrooms are tender and the topping is browned. Serve hot.

CLIVEDEN LOAF

225 g/8 oz mushrooms, chopped
175 g/6 oz onions, peeled and chopped
25 g/1 oz polyunsaturated margarine
1 teaspoon mixed dried sweet herbs
75 g/3 oz Cheddar cheese, grated
1 egg

100 g/4 oz wholemeal breadcrumbs, toasted
TOPPING
15 g/½ oz polyunsaturated margarine

MAKES 1 × 450 g/1 lb loaf
High Fibre

Fry the mushrooms and onions in the margarine until they appear translucent. Remove from the heat and add the mixed herbs and grated cheese. Mix together and bind with the egg.

Line the base and sides of a well-greased 450 g (1 lb) loaf tin with the toasted breadcrumbs. Spoon in the mushroom mixture, cover the top with the remaining breadcrumbs and dot with margarine.

Bake in a preheated moderately hot oven (200°C, 400°F, Gas Mark 6), for 40 minutes.

Turn out and serve hot. Alternatively, wrap in foil, refrigerate and serve with a salad.

CARROT AND ALMOND LOAF WITH TOMATO SAUCE

100 g/4 oz flaked almonds
15 g/½ oz polyunsaturated margarine
1 medium onion, peeled and sliced
2 garlic cloves, peeled and chopped
275 g/10 oz fresh wholemeal breadcrumbs
225 g/8 oz carrots, peeled and grated
2 eggs, beaten
juice of 1 lemon
1 tablespoon chopped parsley
1 teaspoon grated nutmeg
salt and freshly ground black pepper

SAUCE
1 tablespoon vegetable oil
1 medium onion, peeled and sliced
1 garlic clove, peeled and chopped
1 × 400 g (14 oz) can tomatoes
2 tablespoons tomato purée
1 tablespoon chopped fresh basil or 1½
    teaspoons dried basil
salt and freshly ground black pepper

SERVES 8
High Fibre

Grease a 19 × 13 × 9 cm (7½ × 5 × 3½ inch) loaf tin and heat the oven to moderately hot (200°C, 400°F, Gas Mark 6).

Put the almonds into a pan and dry-fry for a few minutes, shaking the pan frequently. Remove from the pan.

Melt the margarine in the pan and fry the onion and garlic for 5 minutes until soft.

In a large bowl, combine the breadcrumbs, carrots and toasted almonds. Add the onion and garlic and stir well. Add the beaten eggs, lemon juice, parsley and nutmeg. Season with salt and pepper and mix thoroughly. Add a little water if more liquid is required, then spoon the mixture into the loaf tin and bake in the oven for 45 minutes or until a sharp knife inserted in the centre comes out clean.

Towards the end of the cooking time, prepare the tomato sauce, heat the oil in a frying pan and gently fry the onion and garlic for about 5 minutes until soft. Add the tomatoes, tomato purée and basil. Season with salt and pepper, stir well and simmer gently until the carrot loaf is cooked. Serve immediately.

CARROT AND ALMOND LOAF WITH TOMATO SAUCE

NUT AND VEGETABLE LOAF

15 g/½ oz polyunsaturated margarine
1 small onion, peeled and chopped
1 small carrot, scraped and chopped
1 celery stick, trimmed and chopped
2 teaspoons tomato purée
225 g/8 oz tomatoes, skinned and chopped
2 eggs
1 teaspoon dried thyme

salt and freshly ground black pepper
100 g/4 oz nuts, chopped or minced
TO GARNISH
onion rings
chopped parsley

SERVES 4
High Fibre

Grease a 20 × 12 cm (8 × 4½ inch) loaf tin and heat the oven to hot (220°C, 425°F, Gas Mark 7).

Melt the margarine and gently fry the onion, carrot and celery until soft, then add the tomato purée and tomatoes and cook for 5 minutes.

Put the eggs into a bowl with the thyme. Season with salt and pepper and beat well. Stir in the nuts and then the vegetable mixture and transfer to the loaf tin. Bake in the oven for 25–30 minutes. Turn out and, if liked, garnish with onion rings and parsley.

HERB AND NUT ROAST

100 g/4 oz hazelnuts
100 g/4 oz wholemeal bread, cubed
25 ml/1 fl oz vegetable oil
450 g/1 lb onions, peeled and chopped
1 tablespoon yeast extract
100 g/4 oz unsalted cashews or peanuts

2 tablespoons chopped parsley
2 tablespoons chopped mixed herbs
salt and freshly ground black pepper

SERVES 4–6
High Fibre   Vegan

Heat the oven to moderate (180°C, 350°F, Gas Mark 4).

Put the hazelnuts into a blender, reserving about 12 whole ones. Add the bread and grind coarsely.

Heat the oil in a large pan, add the onions and fry gently for 10 minutes until soft. Stir in the yeast extract.

Remove from the heat, then stir in the ground hazelnuts and bread, cashews or peanuts and herbs. Season to taste.

Press the mixture into a 900 ml (1½ pint) pie dish or ovenproof casserole. Press the reserved nuts into the top and bake in the oven for 40 minutes until lightly browned on top. Serve hot.

UNDERGROUND HOTPOT

450 g/1 lb potatoes, peeled and thinly sliced
225 g/8 oz onions, peeled and sliced
225 g/8 oz carrots, scraped and sliced
225 g/8 oz parsnips, peeled and sliced
225 g/8 oz Jerusalem artichokes, peeled and sliced
2 celery sticks, trimmed and sliced
100 g/4 oz whole peanuts, shelled

100 g/4 oz mature Cheddar cheese, grated
2 tablespoons chopped rosemary leaves
salt and freshly ground black pepper
300 ml/½ pint Vegetable stock (page 20)

SERVES 4
High Fibre

Heat the oven to moderately hot (190°C, 375°F, Gas Mark 5).

Put half the potato slices in the bottom of a 1.75 litre (3 pint) ovenproof dish. Arrange the remaining vegetables in the dish in layers, sprinkling each layer with the nuts, cheese, rosemary and salt and pepper to taste. Reserve a little cheese for the topping. Finish with a layer of potatoes arranged neatly in circles on top, then pour on the stock and sprinkle with the reserved cheese.

Bake in the oven for 1½ hours until the top is browned and the vegetables are tender when pierced with a skewer. Serve hot.

SOYA BEAN MOUSSAKA

225 g/8 oz soya beans, soaked overnight in cold water
600 ml/1 pint water
3–4 tablespoons vegetable oil
2 onions, peeled and chopped
2 celery sticks, trimmed and sliced
1 large carrot, scraped and sliced
100 g/4 oz mushrooms, trimmed and sliced
4 tomatoes, skinned and chopped
1 tablespoon tomato purée
1 teaspoon dried marjoram
salt and freshly ground black pepper
1 bay leaf

750 g/1½ lb aubergines, thinly sliced
SAUCE
25 g/1 oz polyunsaturated margarine
25 g/1 oz plain wholemeal flour
300 ml/½ pint skimmed milk
50 g/2 oz Cheddar cheese, grated
1 egg, beaten
½ teaspoon made mustard
TO GARNISH
chopped parsley

SERVES 6
High Fibre

Drain the beans, reserving the water. Make up to 1.2 litres/2 pints with more water. Put the beans and liquid into a large pan, then bring to the boil. Skim, then lower the heat, cover and simmer about 2 hours until the beans are just tender. Drain and reserve 300 ml/½ pint cooking liquid.

Heat 1 tablespoon of the oil in a large pan. Add the onions, celery and carrot and fry gently for 5 minutes. Add the mushrooms and fry for a further 2 minutes. Stir in the reserved cooking liquid together with the tomatoes, tomato purée, marjoram and salt and pepper to taste. Bring to the boil, stirring constantly. Add the beans and bay leaf, cover and simmer for 1 hour or until the beans are tender and most of the liquid has been absorbed to give a moist mixture. Discard the bay leaf.

Meanwhile, put the aubergine slices in a colander, sprinkling the layers with salt. Leave for about 1 hour to allow the water to drain off and remove the bitterness. Rinse under cold running water to remove the salt, then pat dry.

Heat the oven to moderate (180°C, 350°F, Gas Mark 4).

Place the aubergine slices in a single layer in the grill pan. Brush lightly with oil and grill for about 5 minutes until lightly browned, turning once. Repeat with any remaining aubergine.

Place one-third of the aubergines in a 1.75 litre (3 pint) ovenproof dish. Cover with half the bean mixture, then another third of the aubergines. Spread the remaining bean mixture on top, then finish with a layer of aubergines.

To make the sauce, melt the margarine in a pan, add the flour and cook for 1–2 minutes, stirring constantly. Remove from the heat and stir in the milk gradually. Return to the heat and bring to the boil, stirring constantly. Simmer for 2 minutes until thick, then stir in half the cheese and the beaten egg. Add the mustard and salt and pepper to taste.

Pour the cheese sauce over the top of the moussaka, then sprinkle with the remaining cheese. Bake in the oven for 30 minutes until the topping is browned. Garnish with parsley and serve hot.

COURGETTE AND TOMATO GOUGÈRE

350 g / 12 oz courgettes, trimmed and sliced
salt and freshly ground black pepper
2 tablespoons vegetable oil
2 medium onions, peeled and chopped
1 green pepper, cored, seeded and sliced
225 g / 8 oz tomatoes, skinned and quartered
1 teaspoon dried oregano
2 teaspoons grated Parmesan cheese
CHOUX PASTE
65 g / 2½ oz wholemeal flour
pinch of salt
50 g / 2 oz polyunsaturated margarine
150 ml / ¼ pint water
2 eggs, beaten

SERVES 3

Put the courgette slices into a colander and sprinkle with salt, then leave them for 15 minutes to remove some of the excess moisture.

Heat the oven to moderately hot (200°C, 400°F, Gas Mark 6). Heat the oil in a large non-stick frying pan, add the onions and cook slowly for 5 minutes. Stir in the green pepper. Rinse and drain the courgettes and add them to the pan. Cook for a further 5 minutes, stirring occasionally. Add the tomatoes, oregano and seasoning. Cook for about 10 minutes until beginning to soften. Leave on one side.

To make the choux paste, sift the flour and salt together on to a sheet of paper, returning the bran retained in the sieve to the flour. Melt the margarine in a saucepan, add the water and bring to the boil.

When bubbling, remove the pan from the heat and immediately add the flour all at once. Beat the mixture until it is smooth and leaves the sides of the pan clean. Allow to cool slightly, then gradually add the eggs, beating well between each addition.

Spoon the mixture around the edge of a shallow 1.2 litre (2 pint) ovenproof dish. Turn the vegetable mixture into the centre and sprinkle over the Parmesan cheese. Cook in the oven for 30–35 minutes until the choux paste is golden brown and well risen. Serve with a salad.

SPINACH AND MUSHROOM ROULADE

225 g/8 oz frozen spinach or 450 g/1 lb fresh
   spinach
4 eggs, separated
salt and freshly ground black pepper
25 g/1 oz grated Parmesan cheese
FILLING
15 g/½ oz polyunsaturated margarine
175 g/6 oz mushrooms, trimmed and sliced

1 tablespoon plain wholemeal flour
150 ml/¼ pint skimmed milk
pinch of grated nutmeg
salt and freshly ground black pepper

SERVES 4
High Fibre

Line a 30 × 20 cm (12 × 8 inch) Swiss roll tin with greaseproof paper and oil lightly, or make a case of the same measurements with foil. Heat the oven to moderately hot (200°C, 400°F, Gas Mark 6).

Cook the spinach with a minimum of water until completely softened. Drain well, chop if using fresh and place in a large bowl. Add the egg yolks and beat them well into the spinach. Season with salt and pepper.

Whisk the egg whites in a large bowl until just holding their shape. Using a metal spoon, quickly fold these into the spinach mixture. Turn the mixture into the prepared tin, sprinkle the Parmesan over and bake in the oven for 10 minutes.

Meanwhile make the filling. Heat the margarine in a saucepan and gently fry the mushrooms until softened. Stir in the flour and cook for a further 1 minute. Gradually stir in the milk and cook until thickened. Stir in the nutmeg, salt and pepper to taste.

Remove the roulade from the oven and turn out on to a sheet of greaseproof paper. Spread the mushroom filling over the surface and gently roll the roulade up. Serve immediately.

CAULIFLOWER CHEESE TIMBALE

450 g/1 lb cauliflower, trimmed and chopped,
   with leaves and stalks finely chopped
1 large onion, peeled and chopped
300 ml/½ pint water
salt
4 eggs, lightly beaten
50 g/2 oz fresh wholemeal breadcrumbs

50 g/2 oz Parmesan cheese, grated
pinch of grated nutmeg
freshly ground white pepper
300 ml/½ pint skimmed milk

SERVES 4

Heat the oven to moderate (180°C, 350°F, Gas Mark 4).

Put the cauliflower and onion into a large pan with the water and salt. Bring to the boil, then lower the heat, cover and simmer for about 10 minutes until the cauliflower is just tender. Drain.

Put the eggs into a bowl with the breadcrumbs, cheese and nutmeg and season with salt and pepper. Mix well. Heat the milk, but do not allow to boil, then stir into the egg mixture.

Put the cauliflower into a 1.5 litre (2½ pint) ovenproof dish or greased ring mould. Pour the egg mixture over the cauliflower. Stand the dish or mould in a roasting pan, half-filled with hot water and bake in the oven for 45 minutes or until the custard is set and a skewer comes out clean when inserted in the centre.

Serve straight from the dish or mould, or leave to stand for a few minutes, then turn out on to a warmed serving platter. Serve hot with Fresh tomato sauce (page 52). The timbale can also be served cold, in which case it should be left to cool in the dish or mould before turning out on to a serving platter.

Vegetable Dishes

BRUSSELS SPROUTS WITH CHESTNUTS

1 kg/2 lb Brussels sprouts, trimmed
225 g/8 oz chestnuts
salt
2 teaspoons vegetable oil
grated rind and juice of ½ lemon

SERVES 6
Low Fat   High Fibre   Vegan

Cut a small cross in the base of each Brussels sprout stalk so they cook evenly.

Snip the tops of the chestnuts with a pair of scissors. Put them into a saucepan, cover with cold water and bring to the boil. Boil for 3 minutes, then remove the chestnuts one at a time. Allow to cool a little and peel off both the outer and inner skins.

Cook the sprouts in boiling, salted water for 15 minutes, adding the peeled chestnuts for the last 5 minutes of cooking time. Drain well. Heat the oil in the same pan. Add the lemon rind and juice, return the sprouts and chestnuts to the pan and toss well in the oil before serving.

BROCCOLI AND ALMONDS

450 g/1 lb broccoli spears, trimmed
1 tablespoon vegetable oil
1 onion, peeled and sliced
1 garlic clove, peeled and crushed
50 g/2 oz blanched almonds
5 tomatoes, skinned and chopped

salt and freshly ground black pepper
1 tablespoon chopped parsley

SERVES 4
High Fibre   Vegan

Cook the broccoli spears in boiling, salted water for about 15 minutes until just tender.

Heat the oil in a pan and gently fry the onion, garlic and almonds until the onion is soft and the almonds are beginning to brown. Remove the almonds and drain on absorbent kitchen paper. Stir the tomatoes into the onions and heat through. Season with salt and pepper to taste.

Drain the broccoli and place in a heated serving dish. Spoon the sauce over the broccoli and sprinkle with the browned almonds and chopped parsley. Serve hot.

POTATO AND LEEK LAYER

450 g / 1 lb potatoes, peeled and thinly sliced
225 g / 8 oz leeks, trimmed and thinly sliced
1/4 teaspoon grated nutmeg
salt and freshly ground black pepper
300 ml / 1/2 pint skimmed milk

SERVES 4
Low Fat

Heat the oven to moderately hot (190°C, 375°F, Gas Mark 5).

Arrange the potatoes and leeks in layers in a 1.2 litre (2 pint) casserole. Sprinkle the layers with nutmeg, salt and pepper and finish with a layer of potatoes with a few leeks in the centre. Pour over the milk and cover. Bake in the oven for 1 hour.

Uncover and cook for a further 30 minutes until the potatoes are browned and tender, and most of the milk has been absorbed. Serve hot.

DANISH RED CABBAGE

1 tablespoon vegetable oil
1 medium red cabbage, trimmed and finely
    shredded
1 large onion, peeled and finely sliced
1 large cooking apple, skinned, cored and sliced
1 tablespoon caraway seeds
2 tablespoons wine vinegar

salt and freshly ground black pepper
2 tablespoons Vegetable stock (page 20)
TO GARNISH
chopped parsley

SERVES 4
Low Fat   High Fibre   Vegan

Heat the oil in a large pan. Add the cabbage, onion, apple, caraway seeds, vinegar, salt, pepper and stock. Stir well and cover with a close-fitting lid.

Allow to cook gently for 40–45 minutes, stirring or shaking from time to time. Garnish with parsley. *Illustrated on page 65.*

FENOUIL À LA GRÈCQUE

2 tablespoons vegetable oil
2 tablespoons water
2 tomatoes, skinned and chopped
6 coriander seeds
1 bay leaf
sprig of thyme
salt and freshly ground black pepper

3–4 fennel bulbs, trimmed and quartered
juice of 1/2 lemon
TO GARNISH
chopped parsley

SERVES 4
Vegan

Put the oil, water, tomatoes, coriander seeds, bay leaf and thyme into a saucepan. Season with salt and pepper. Bring to the boil and simmer for 3–4 minutes.

Toss the fennel in lemon juice and add to the pan. Cook gently until the fennel is tender but not too soft.

Using a slotted spoon transfer the fennel to a serving dish.

Cook the sauce quickly over a high heat until it starts to thicken. Pour over the fennel and allow to cool.

FENOUIL À LA GRÈCQUE

CHINESE STIR-FRIED VEGETABLES

1 tablespoon vegetable oil
1 large onion, peeled and chopped
1 garlic clove, peeled and crushed
1 tablespoon peeled and grated fresh root ginger
50 g/2 oz mushrooms, trimmed and sliced
450 g/1 lb mangetout, topped and tailed
450 g/1 lb Chinese leaves or other cabbage,
  trimmed and shredded

100 g/4 oz bean-sprouts
50 g/2 oz peanuts, shelled
1 tablespoon soy sauce
5 tablespoons stock or water
salt and freshly ground black pepper

SERVES 4
High Fibre   Vegan

Heat the oil in a wok or large frying pan. Add the onion, garlic, ginger and mushrooms and fry briskly for 3 minutes, stirring constantly.

Add the mangetout and Chinese leaves and fry for a further 2 minutes, stirring constantly.

Add the remaining ingredients and stir-fry over moderate heat for about 5 minutes until the vegetables are tender but still crisp, and most of the liquid has evaporated. Taste and adjust the seasoning and serve immediately.

VEGETABLE PILAFF

PILAFF
1 tablespoon vegetable oil
1 onion, peeled and chopped
225 g/8 oz long-grain rice
600 ml/1 pint Vegetable stock (page 20)
1 cinnamon stick or pinch of ground cinnamon
1 bay leaf
salt and freshly ground black pepper
VEGETABLES
2 tablespoons vegetable oil
1 onion, peeled and sliced
1 garlic clove, peeled and crushed (optional)

450 g/1 lb courgettes, trimmed and sliced
1 green pepper, cored, seeded and diced
100 g/4 oz button mushrooms, trimmed
450 g/1 lb tomatoes, skinned and roughly
  chopped
1 tablespoon chopped fresh herbs (oregano,
  marjoram, basil and parsley) or 1 teaspoon
  dried mixed herbs

SERVES 4
Vegan

To make the pilaff, heat the oil in a saucepan and fry the onion for 5 minutes. Add the rice and cook, stirring, for 1 minute. Pour in the stock and add the remaining ingredients. Bring to the boil, stirring occasionally. Cover the pan and simmer gently for 15–20 minutes until the rice is cooked and all the stock has been absorbed.

Meanwhile, prepare the vegetables. Heat the oil in a saucepan and fry the onion, garlic and courgettes for about 5 minutes, stirring occasionally until the vegetables are lightly browned. Add the pepper and mushrooms and fry for 2 minutes. Add the tomatoes with the herbs, salt and pepper. Cook for 10–15 minutes, stirring occasionally until the tomatoes are reduced to a pulp and the courgettes are just tender.

Transfer the pilaff to a warm serving dish and pour over the vegetables. Serve hot.

DANISH RED CABBAGE (PAGE 62)

ALMOND AND HERB RICE RING

225 g/8 oz long grain or medium grain rice
600 ml/1 pint water
salt
4 tablespoons chopped fresh mixed herbs
   (chives, oregano, thyme, basil and parsley)
   or 2 tablespoons dried mixed herbs
50 g/2 oz split almonds

SERVES 4–6
Vegan

Heat the oven to moderate (180°C, 350°F, Gas Mark 4).

Cook the rice in the boiling salted water for 10 minutes. Add the chopped herbs and cook for a further 5 minutes until the rice is just tender. Drain thoroughly.

Place the almonds on a baking sheet in the preheated oven for about 5 minutes, until golden brown.

Lightly grease a 900 ml (1½ pint) ring mould. Then place the split almonds in the base of the ring.

Spoon the rice into the mould, pressing it down firmly with the back of the spoon. Cover and bake in the oven for 20 minutes until heated through.

Cover the mould with a serving plate, invert and remove the mould. Serve at once.

HERBED RICE

100 g/4 oz long-grain brown rice
salt and freshly ground black pepper
2 tablespoons vegetable oil
2 teaspoons white wine vinegar
squeeze of lemon juice
2 tablespoons chopped parsley

2 tablespoons chopped chives
1 tablespoon chopped dill
1 tablespoon chopped tarragon

SERVES 4
High Fibre   Vegan

This can be served with hard-boiled eggs, or other vegetarian dishes.

Cook the rice in a saucepan of boiling, salted water for 35–40 minutes or until tender, then drain well. While the rice is still hot, season with salt and pepper and add the oil, vinegar, and lemon juice.

When the rice has cooled, stir in the chopped herbs.

HERB RISOTTO

1 tablespoon vegetable oil
1 shallot, peeled and chopped
225 g/8 oz brown rice
about 750 ml/1¼ pints hot Vegetable stock
   (page 20)
pinch of saffron
1 bay leaf, crushed
12 sage leaves, finely chopped

12 sprigs thyme, finely chopped
12 tarragon leaves, finely chopped
12 marjoram leaves, finely chopped
salt

SERVES 4
High Fibre   Vegan

Heat the oil in a heavy saucepan and cook the shallot until soft. Add the rice to the pan and stir around until coated with fat, then pour on 400 ml/14 fl oz of the stock. Cover the pan and simmer gently until almost all the liquid is absorbed.

Add the saffron, bay leaf and herbs to 175 ml/6 fl oz of the stock and pour it over the rice. Cover again, and cook gently until the stock is absorbed. If the rice is tender, season with salt and pepper and serve, otherwise add the remaining stock and continue to simmer until cooked.

FRENCH-STYLE MANGETOUT

15 g/½ oz polyunsaturated margarine
1 bunch (about 8) spring onions, trimmed and cut into 5 cm/2 inch lengths
500 g/1¼ lb mangetout, topped and tailed
300 ml/½ pint well-flavoured Vegetable stock (page 20)
1 bouquet garni
salt

1 tablespoon cornflour
2 tablespoons water
1 firm lettuce, trimmed and cut into 8 wedges
4 tablespoons low-fat soft cheese
1 tablespoon green peppercorns, drained

SERVES 4
High Fibre

If you cannot buy mangetout, use freshly shelled peas.

Melt the margarine in a pan, add the spring onions and cook for 2 minutes without browning. Add the mangetout, stock and bouquet garni. Season with salt, bring to the boil, then lower the heat and simmer for 10–12 minutes until the vegetables are just tender.

Discard the bouquet garni. Blend the cornflour with the water and stir into the vegetables. Bring to the boil, stirring constantly. Lower the heat and simmer for 2 minutes, then add the lettuce and soft cheese. Heat through gently for 1–2 minutes, then add the peppercorns. Taste and adjust seasoning. Serve at once.

COURGETTES PROVENCAL

450 g/1 lb courgettes, sliced
4 tomatoes, sliced
1 small onion, peeled and grated
2 tablespoons chopped parsley
1 tablespoon thyme leaves

salt and freshly ground black pepper
5 tablespoons Vegetable stock (page 20)

SERVES 4
Low Fat   Vegan

This dish may also be cooked on top of the stove. Reserve half the parsley and put all the other ingredients into a large saucepan. Cover and cook gently for 10 minutes until just tender, stirring occasionally. Garnish with the reserved parsley.

Heat the oven to moderate (180°C, 350°F, Gas Mark 4).

Arrange the courgettes and tomatoes in layers in a baking dish or casserole, sprink-ling each layer with the onion, half the parsley, the thyme, and salt and pepper to taste. Pour in the stock.

Cover and bake in the oven for 30–40 minutes until the courgettes are tender but not soft.

Taste and adjust the seasoning. Sprinkle with the remaining parsley and serve hot or cold.

CHICORY IN MUSTARD SAUCE

salt
150 ml / ¼ pint water
juice of 1 lemon
4 heads chicory, trimmed
1 tablespoon vegetable oil
scant 1 tablespoon plain wholemeal flour

150 ml / ¼ pint Vegetable stock (page 20)
scant 2 tablespoons made mild mustard
1 tablespoon chopped dill

SERVES 4
Low Fat   Vegan

Salt the water, add the lemon juice and bring to the boil. Add the chicory heads, lower the heat and cook for about 10 minutes. Drain, reserving the cooking liquid.

Heat the oil in a small pan, stir in the flour and cook until golden. Gradually add the reserved cooking liquid and the stock, stirring constantly. Add the mustard and bring to the boil, stirring constantly. Add the par-cooked chicory and cook for a further 10 minutes over a very low heat until just tender.

Transfer to a warmed serving dish and sprinkle with the chopped dill. Serve immediately.

LEEKS NIÇOISE

6 leeks, trimmed and cleaned
1 × 200 g (7 oz) can tomatoes, chopped
1 teaspoon chopped fresh basil
1 garlic clove, peeled and crushed
salt and freshly ground black pepper
TO GARNISH
chopped parsley

SERVES 4
Low Fat   High Fibre   Vegan

Put the leeks in a deep pan. Add the tomatoes with their juice, the chopped basil and the garlic. Season to taste with salt and pepper. Bring to the boil, lower the heat and cover. Simmer for about 20 minutes, or until the leeks are tender, stirring occasionally.

Sprinkle over the chopped parsley and serve immediately.

LEFT: CHICORY IN MUSTARD SAUCE;
RIGHT: SPINACH PANCAKES (PAGE 21)

EASTERN MOOLI

1 tablespoon vegetable oil
1 onion, peeled and sliced
2 tablespoons chopped fresh mint
1 teaspoon ground turmeric
¼ teaspoon chilli powder
450 g / 1 lb mooli, peeled and cut into 2.5 cm /
  inch pieces

salt
3 tablespoons hot water
1 teaspoon garam masala
1 tablespoon lemon juice

SERVES 3
Low Fat   Vegan

Mooli, sometimes called white radish, is a vegetable imported from East Africa.

Heat the oil in a frying pan. Add the onion and fry gently until beginning to soften. Add the mint, turmeric and chilli powder. Season with salt, then stir in the mooli so it is well covered. Add the water, cover and simmer for 20 minutes, shaking the frying pan occasionally.

Sprinkle with the garam masala and lemon juice. Replace the lid and cook for a further 10 minutes or until the mooli is tender. Serve with rice or chappatis, or if served as an accompanying vegetable to curry, this quantity will serve 4–6.

Light Meals & Snacks

PIPÉRADE

1 tablespoon vegetable oil
100 g/4 oz onion, peeled and sliced
100 g/4 oz red or green peppers, cored, seeded
   and sliced
2 garlic cloves, peeled and crushed
3 large tomatoes, skinned, seeded and chopped
salt and freshly ground black pepper

4 eggs
2 tablespoons skimmed milk
TO GARNISH
chopped parsley

SERVES 4

Heat the oil and gently fry the onion, until almost soft. Add the peppers and, after 5 minutes, the garlic and tomatoes. Season with salt and pepper and simmer until all the ingredients are soft and most of the liquid from the tomatoes has evaporated.

Beat the eggs and milk in a small pan and scramble lightly. Turn the vegetables on to a heated dish, spread the eggs on top and fork a little of the vegetables into the edges of the egg. Sprinkle with chopped parsley and serve surrounded with small triangles of wholemeal toast spread with garlic-flavoured margarine.

JERUSALEM COCOTTES

450 g/1 lb Jerusalem artichokes, scrubbed
salt
150 ml/¼ pint plain unsweetened yogurt
freshly ground white pepper
4 eggs

TO GARNISH
chopped parsley

SERVES 4

Heat the oven to moderate (180°C, 350°F, Gas Mark 4).

Cook the artichokes in boiling salted water for about 20 minutes or until tender. Peel off the skins and mash the artichokes well. Stir in the yogurt and season with salt and pepper. Alternatively, work the ingredients to a smooth purée in a blender.

Spread the mixture into four individual ovenproof dishes or one large baking dish. Make four hollows for the eggs and crack an egg into each hollow.

Bake in the oven for 10–15 minutes or until the eggs are just set. Garnish with parsley and serve hot.

FLORENTINE EGGS

750 g / 1½ lb fresh leaf spinach, trimmed
salt
50 g / 2 oz polyunsaturated margarine
50 g / 2 oz plain flour
600 ml / 1 pint skimmed milk
50 g / 2 oz mature Cheddar cheese, grated

freshly ground black pepper
4 eggs

SERVES 4
High Fibre

Put the spinach leaves into a large pan with a minimum of water. Season with salt and cook, uncovered, for 10–15 minutes until completely softened. Drain well and chop.

Melt the margarine in a saucepan. Stir in the flour, then gradually blend in the milk to make a smooth consistency. Bring to the boil over a medium heat, stirring constantly and cook for 3–4 minutes. Mix in half the cheese and season with salt and pepper to taste.

Lower the eggs into boiling water and boil for just 3 minutes so they are still soft in the centre. Immediately plunge the eggs into cold water.

Stir a quarter of the sauce into the spinach and divide the mixture between four individual dishes. Carefully peel the shells off the eggs and place one egg in the centre of each dish. Spoon over the rest of the sauce. Sprinkle the tops with the remaining cheese and put under the grill for about 10 minutes. Serve at once.

PISSALADIÈRE

175 g / 6 oz wholemeal flour
½ teaspoon ground cinnamon (optional)
pinch of salt
75 g / 3 oz polyunsaturated margarine
1 egg yolk
FILLING
3 tablespoons vegetable oil
450 g / 1 lb onions, peeled and thinly sliced
2 garlic cloves, peeled and crushed

450 g / 1 lb tomatoes, skinned and chopped
1 bouquet garni
2 tablespoons tomato purée
freshly ground black pepper
50 g / 2 oz stoned black olives

SERVES 4–6
High Fibre

Sift the flour, cinnamon, if used, and salt together into a bowl. Add the margarine and rub it in until the mixture resembles breadcrumbs. Mix in the egg yolk, adding a little cold water if necessary to make a fairly firm dough.

Knead the dough for a few seconds on a floured surface until smooth. Roll it out and use to line a 20 cm (8 inch) plain flan ring. Leave in a cool place for 15 minutes.

Heat the oven to moderately hot (200°C, 400°F, Gas Mark 6).

To make the filling, heat the oil in a frying pan, add the onions and garlic and fry gently for about 10 minutes. Stir in the tomatoes, bouquet garni and tomato purée. Season with salt and pepper and bring the mixture to the boil. Lower the heat and simmer, uncovered, for about 40 minutes, then remove the bouquet garni.

Line the flan ring with greaseproof paper, weight down with baking beans and bake blind in the oven for 15 minutes. Remove the paper and beans.

Spoon the tomato mixture into the flan case. Arrange the olives on top and return to the oven for a further 20 minutes, brushing the olives with a little extra oil if they become dry.

LEFT: MEDITERRANEAN LENTIL STEW (PAGE 115); RIGHT: ITALIAN BEAN SOUP

ITALIAN BEAN SOUP

*225 g/8 oz dried white beans (haricot or butter
  beans), soaked overnight in cold water*
1 large onion, peeled and chopped
1 garlic clove, peeled and crushed (optional)
1 celery stick, trimmed and sliced
1 large carrot, peeled and sliced
4 tomatoes, skinned and chopped
finely grated rind and juice of ½ lemon

1 bay leaf
salt and freshly ground black pepper
TO GARNISH
2 tablespoons chopped parsley (optional)

SERVES 6
Low Fat   High Fibre   Vegan

Drain the beans, reserving the water. Make up to 1.2 litres/2 pints with more water. Put the beans and liquid into a large pan, then add all the remaining ingredients. Bring to the boil, then lower the heat, cover and simmer for 1–1½ hours until the beans are tender, adding more water if necessary. Discard the bay leaf.

Transfer about half the beans and some of the liquid into a blender and then work into a smooth purée.

Return the purée to the pan and bring to the boil, stirring constantly. Taste and adjust the seasoning, and add more liquid if the soup is too thick. Sprinkle with parsley if liked, and serve hot.

FRENCH BEAN AND TOMATO CASSEROLE

2 tablespoons sesame seeds
750 g / 1½ lb French beans, topped and tailed
250 g / 8 oz courgettes, trimmed and sliced
salt
15 g / ½ oz polyunsaturated margarine
2 onions, peeled and sliced
1–2 garlic cloves, peeled and sliced
500 g / 1¼ lb tomatoes, skinned, seeded and
  chopped

2 spring onions, trimmed and chopped
freshly ground black pepper
250 g / 8 oz Mozzarella cheese, thinly sliced
TO GARNISH
few sprigs of fresh herbs (optional)

SERVES 6

Dry-fry the sesame seeds for about 1 minute until lightly browned, shaking the pan frequently. Set aside.

Blanch the beans and courgettes in boiling, salted water for 3 minutes. Drain.

Melt the margarine in a pan, add the onions and garlic and fry gently for 5 minutes until soft. Stir in the tomatoes, bring to the boil and cook, uncovered, for 15 minutes until thickened. Stir in the spring onions and season with salt and pepper, then add the drained beans and courgettes.

Lightly grease an ovenproof dish or foil container and heat the oven to moderate (180°C, 350°F, Gas Mark 4).

Spoon a layer of bean and tomato mixture into the bottom of the ovenproof dish or foil container. Cover with a layer of cheese, then another layer of bean and tomato mixture. Continue with these layers until all the ingredients are used up, finishing with a layer of cheese.

Bake for 30–35 minutes. Sprinkle over the sesame seeds, return to the oven and bake for a further 5 minutes. Serve hot, garnished with sprigs of fresh herbs if liked.

TOMATO AND OLIVE PIZZA

1 × recipe Pizza dough (page 49)
TOPPING
1 tablespoon vegetable oil
275 g / 10 oz onions, peeled and chopped
350 g / 12 oz tomatoes, skinned and chopped
½ teaspoon oregano
1 tablespoon tomato purée

50 g / 2 oz Cheddar cheese, grated
salt and freshly ground black pepper
15 black olives, halved and stoned

SERVES 4–6
High Fibre

On a lightly floured surface, roll out the dough to a 20 cm (8 inch) diameter circle and carefully transfer it to a large greased baking sheet. Heat the oven to hot (220°C, 425°F, Gas Mark 7).

To make the topping: heat the oil in a non-stick frying pan, add the onions and gently fry for about 5 minutes until soft. Stir in the tomatoes and oregano and cook rapidly for 10 minutes or until thick. Season and add the tomato purée.

Spread the mixture over the pizza base to within 1 cm (½ inch) of the edges. Sprinkle over the cheese, then arrange the black olive halves on top. Cook in the oven for 12 minutes until the base is cooked and the cheese golden brown.

MUSHROOM AND PEPPER PIZZA

1 × recipe Pizza dough (page 49)
2 tablespoons vegetable oil
225 g/8 oz onions, peeled and sliced
1 red pepper
1 green pepper
1 garlic clove, peeled and crushed

100 g/4 oz mushrooms, trimmed and sliced
salt and freshly ground black pepper
50 g/2 oz Cheddar cheese, grated

SERVES 4
High Fibre

Grease a large baking sheet and pre-heat the oven to hot (220°C, 425°F, Gas Mark 7).

On a lightly floured surface, roll out the pastry to a 20 cm (8 inch) diameter circle and carefully transfer to the baking sheet.

Heat the oil in a frying pan, add the onions and fry gently until softened.

Cut 2 or 3 rings from each pepper, then core and seed the remainder and chop the flesh roughly. Add the chopped peppers to the onion with the garlic and mushrooms and cook for a further 5 minutes.

Spread the mixture over the pastry base. Cover with the cheese, garnish with the pepper rings and cook in the oven for 12 minutes or until the base is cooked.

WATERCRESS AND SPRING ONION QUICHE

1 × recipe Wholemeal shortcrust pastry (pages 106–7)
FILLING
15 g/½ oz polyunsaturated margarine
8 large spring onions, trimmed and chopped
1 large bunch watercress, trimmed and roughly chopped
3 eggs
150 ml/¼ pint skimmed milk
1 teaspoon French mustard

pinch of dried mixed herbs
50 g/2 oz mature Cheddar cheese, grated
salt
cayenne pepper
TO GARNISH
few watercress sprigs
few spring onions, trimmed and sliced

SERVES 4

Make the pastry according to the recipe on pages 106–7, then roll out and use to line a 20 cm (8 inch) flan ring about 2.5 cm (1 inch) deep, placed on a baking sheet. Chill in the refrigerator for 30 minutes.

To make the filling, melt the margarine in a pan, add the spring onions and fry gently for 3 minutes without browning. Stir in the watercress and cook for 1 minute until just soft, then remove from the heat and leave to cool.

Heat the oven to moderately hot (200°C, 400°F, Gas Mark 6).

Beat the eggs, milk, mustard and herbs together in a bowl. Stir in the cheese, then season to taste with salt and cayenne pepper.

Prick the base and sides of the dough.

Line with foil and weight down with baking beans. Bake blind for 10 minutes, then remove the foil and beans and return to the oven for a further 5 minutes. Spoon the spring onions and watercress over the base, pour over the egg and milk mixture and bake in the oven for 25 minutes, until the filling is well risen and golden brown. Leave to cool. Serve garnished with watercress and spring onions.

BEANS AND EGGS AU GRATIN

450 g / 1 lb shelled broad beans, fresh or frozen
salt
2–3 hard-boiled eggs, sliced
40 g / 1½ oz polyunsaturated margarine
40 g / 1½ oz plain wholemeal flour
450 ml / ¾ pint skimmed milk
cayenne pepper

TOPPING
25 g / 1 oz fresh wholemeal breadcrumbs
50 g / 2 oz mature Cheddar cheese, grated

SERVES 6
High Fibre

Heat the oven to hot (220°C, 425°F, Gas Mark 7).

Cook the beans in boiling salted water until just soft. Drain. Layer the beans and eggs in an ovenproof dish, starting and ending with a layer of beans.

Melt the margarine in a pan and stir in the flour, then gradually blend in the milk. Bring to the boil, stirring constantly and cook for 3–4 minutes. Season with salt and cayenne pepper and pour over the beans.

For the topping, sprinkle the breadcrumbs and cheese over the sauce. Bake in the oven for 15 minutes or until the topping is browned and crisp.

WHOLEMEAL VEGETABLE PASTIES

100 g / 4 oz wholemeal flour
100 g / 4 oz plain flour
salt
100 g / 4 oz polyunsaturated margarine
2–3 tablespoons water
FILLING
100 g / 4 oz shelled broad beans
225 g / 8 oz turnips, peeled and diced
225 g / 8 oz carrots, scraped and grated

2 tablespoons chopped fresh chives
2 tablespoons curd cheese
2 tablespoons plain unsweetened yogurt
salt and freshly ground black pepper
beaten egg, to glaze

SERVES 4
High Fibre

Sift the flours and a pinch of salt together into a bowl. Rub in the fat until the mixture resembles breadcrumbs. Stir in sufficient water to make a fairly stiff dough. Turn the dough on to a floured surface and knead until smooth. Wrap in greaseproof paper and chill for 30 minutes.

To make the filling, cook the beans and turnips in boiling salted water for 10 minutes or until just tender. Drain well, then stir in the carrots, chives, curd cheese and yogurt. Season with salt and pepper and leave on one side to cool.

Heat the oven to moderately hot (200°C, 400°F, Gas Mark 6).

On a floured surface, roll out the dough to a 3 mm (⅛ inch) thickness and cut out four 15 cm (6 inch) circles, using a saucer as a guide. Divide the filling between the pastry rounds. Moisten the edges, then lift them up over the filling to enclose it completely and form the shape of a Cornish pasty. Seal the edges, scallop them and brush all over with the beaten egg. Make a small air vent in the top of each pasty, then cook in the oven for 25–30 minutes or until golden brown. Serve warm or cold.

VEGETABLE LASAGNE

100 g/4 oz green lasagne
1 teaspoon vegetable oil
450 g/1 lb spinach, trimmed, or 225 g/8 oz
    chopped frozen spinach
225 g/8 oz cottage cheese
100 g/4 oz chopped walnuts
2 tablespoons grated Parmesan cheese
1 quantity Thick tomato sauce (page 52)

SAUCE
50 g/2 oz polyunsaturated margarine
50 g/2 oz plain wholemeal flour
600 ml/1 pint skimmed milk
100 g/4 oz Cheddar cheese, grated
salt and freshly ground black pepper

SERVES 4–6
High Fibre

Grease a shallow rectangular or square ovenproof dish and heat the oven to moderately hot (200°C, 400°F, Gas Mark 6).

Place the lasagne in a large saucepan of boiling salted water with the oil added to separate the pasta and cook for about 12 minutes. Drain and drape the pasta pieces around a mixing bowl to prevent them sticking together.

Cook the spinach with a minimum of boiling salted water until completely softened. Drain and finely chop. If using frozen spinach, cook according to the instructions on the packet. Combine the spinach, cottage cheese and walnuts together to make a thick paste.

To make the cheese sauce, melt the margarine in a saucepan, add the flour and cook for 1 minute. Remove from the heat and gradually add the milk. Bring to the boil, stirring until thickened, then add the cheese and salt and pepper to taste.

Line the ovenproof dish with half the lasagne. Layer the Thick tomato sauce, cheese sauce, spinach mixture and remaining lasagne, ending with a layer of cheese sauce. Sprinkle the top with Parmesan cheese and bake in the oven for 30 minutes. Serve immediately.

FETTUCINE WITH COURGETTES AND MUSHROOMS

1 tablespoon vegetable oil
1 medium onion, peeled and sliced
1 garlic clove, peeled and chopped
450 g/1 lb courgettes, trimmed and grated
225 g/8 oz button mushrooms, trimmed and
    sliced
100 g/4 oz curd cheese
85 ml/3 fl oz skimmed milk

450 g/1 lb fettucine
½ teaspoon grated nutmeg
salt and freshly ground black pepper
TO GARNISH
1 tablespoon chopped fresh parsley

SERVES 6

Heat the oil in a heavy frying pan and gently cook the onion and garlic until soft. Add the courgettes and the mushrooms, mixing well together. Cook gently, stirring occasionally for about 10 minutes.

Cook the fettucine in boiling, salted water. Boil for about 7 minutes, until just al dente, then drain.

Whisk the skimmed milk into the curd cheese, then add to the courgette and mushroom mixture with the nutmeg. Season with salt and pepper. Combine with the fettucine and serve immediately, garnished with chopped parsley.

FROM TOP: VEGETABLE LASAGNE, FETTUCINE WITH COURGETTES AND MUSHROOMS

AUBERGINE CASSEROLE

450 g / 1 lb aubergine, cut into 1 cm / ½ inch
   thick slices
600 ml / 1 pint Vegetable stock (page 20)
2 teaspoons vegetable oil
100 g / 4 oz onions, finely chopped
2 garlic cloves, chopped
2 × 400 g (14 oz) cans tomatoes

¼ teaspoon dried oregano
¼ teaspoon dried basil
salt and freshly ground black pepper
175 g / 6 oz Mozzarella cheese, sliced
25 g / 1 oz Cheddar cheese, finely grated

SERVES 4

Place the aubergine slices in a large pan, cover with boiling Vegetable stock. Simmer for 10 minutes and drain.

Heat the oil in a thick frying pan and cook the onions and garlic in it until lightly coloured. Add the tomatoes, herbs and seasoning and cook, stirring occasionally, for about 30 minutes.

Heat the oven to moderate (180°C, 350°F, Gas Mark 4).

Place alternate layers of aubergine, tomatoes and cheese in a large casserole, finishing with a layer of Mozzarella.

Bake in the oven for 30 minutes. Serve with a curly endive salad.

CRACKED WHEAT DIANE

100 g / 4 oz cracked wheat, soaked for 1 hour in
   cold water
50 g / 2 oz onions, finely chopped
1 teaspoon vegetable oil
1 teaspoon cumin
100 ml / 3½ fl oz Vegetable stock (page 20)
100 ml / 3½ fl oz orange juice
1 tablespoon sherry

25 g / 1 oz sultanas
grated rind of ½ orange
25 g / 1 oz chopped walnuts or peanuts
salt and freshly ground black pepper

SERVES 4
Low Fat   High Fibre   Vegan

Fry the onions in the oil in a non-stick pan with the cumin until lightly browned. Then transfer to a large pan with the stock, orange juice, sherry, sultanas and orange rind and bring to the boil. Drain the

strained cracked wheat and add. Simmer. stirring occasionally for 2 minutes. Add the chopped walnuts or peanuts, reheat and serve immediately.

STUFFED MUSHROOMS

3–4 tablespoons olive oil
8 flat mushrooms (about 6 cm / 2½ inch
   diameter), trimmed and stalks cut level with
   caps
350 g / 12 oz tomatoes, skinned and finely
   chopped
1 garlic clove, peeled and crushed

1 bunch spring onions, trimmed and thinly sliced
3 tablespoons chopped chives
salt and freshly ground black pepper
1½ teaspoons lemon juice

SERVES 4
Vegan

Heat the oven to moderate (180°C, 350°F, Gas Mark 4). Oil a baking sheet and lay the mushrooms on it, stalk side uppermost. Brush a little olive oil over each one and bake in the oven for 20 minutes. Remove and leave to cool.

Pile the tomatoes, garlic and spring onions together on a chopping board and chop until reduced to a purée. Put into a bowl, stir in the chopped chives, and season with salt and pepper. Add 1 tablespoon of the olive oil and the lemon juice. Pile a little of the mixture on top of each of the cooled mushroom caps.

Serve as a first course or as part of a selection of vegetable dishes.

MEXICORN PANCAKE MEDLEY

8 Wholemeal pancakes (page 106), kept warm
FILLING
15 g/½ oz polyunsaturated margarine
2 celery sticks, trimmed and chopped
2 tablespoons plain wholemeal flour
150 ml/¼ pint skimmed milk
1 × 350 g (12 oz) can sweet corn kernels, drained
2 tomatoes, skinned and chopped

50 g/2 oz shelled walnuts, chopped
1 tablespoon chopped chives
salt and freshly ground black pepper
50 g/2 oz Cheddar cheese, grated
TO GARNISH
watercress sprigs

SERVES 4
High Fibre

To make the filling, melt the margarine in a saucepan, add the celery and fry gently for 5 minutes. Stir in the flour and cook, stirring, until thickened. Add the remaining ingredients, except the cheese, and season with salt and pepper. Stir over low heat until the mixture is thoroughly heated through. Remove from the heat and stir in the cheese.

Divide the mixture between the pancakes and roll up. Arrange in a warm shallow serving dish. Garnish with watercress and serve immediately.

PAN HAGGERTY

2 tablespoons vegetable oil
450 g/1 lb potatoes, peeled and thinly sliced
salt and freshly ground black pepper
75 g/3 oz mature Cheddar cheese, grated
225 g/8 oz onions, peeled and thinly sliced

SERVES 4

Heat the oil in a heavy-based non-stick frying pan about 20 cm (8 inches) in diameter. Remove the pan from the heat, and arrange half the potatoes overlapping in the bottom of the pan. Sprinkle with a little salt and pepper, then cover with the cheese. Add a layer of onions, more salt and pepper, then make a final layer of potatoes.

Cover the pan and cook over a medium heat for 20 minutes or until the potatoes on the bottom are brown. Invert the mixture on to a plate, then slip it back into the pan to brown the other side and complete the cooking. This will take about another 20 minutes. Serve the pan haggerty with a tomato salad, if liked.

BROCCOLI CASSEROLE

750 ml / 1¼ pints Vegetable stock (page 20)
450 g / 1 lb broccoli, divided into florets
pinch of grated nutmeg
1 tablespoon chopped herbs (chives, parsley or
    thyme)

3 eggs
1 tablespoon skimmed milk
1 tablespoon grated Parmesan cheese

SERVES 4

Grease an ovenproof casserole and heat the oven to moderately hot (200°C, 400°F, Gas Mark 6).

Bring the stock to the boil in a large pan, add the cauliflower and nutmeg. Bring back to the boil, lower the heat, cover and cook gently for 10 minutes. Drain and place in the dish. Sprinkle with the chopped herbs.

Beat the eggs with the milk and Parmesan cheese and pour over the cauliflower. Cook in the oven for about 20 minutes or until the egg custard has set.

SPINACH RAMEKINS

25 g / 1 oz Outline or similar low-fat spread
1 small onion, peeled and chopped
4 tablespoons spinach purée
50 g / 2 oz Edam cheese, grated
4 eggs, beaten
pinch of grated nutmeg

salt and freshly ground black pepper
300 ml / ½ pint skimmed milk
50 g / 2 oz fresh wholemeal breadcrumbs

SERVES 4
High Fibre

Lightly grease four ramekin dishes and heat the oven to moderate (180°C, 350°F, Gas Mark 4).

Melt the low-fat spread in a pan and gently fry the onion until soft, then place in a bowl with the spinach, cheese and eggs. Season with nutmeg and salt and pepper.

Heat the milk until almost boiling and beat into the mixture with the breadcrumbs. Pour into the ramekin dishes. Stand the ramekins in a roasting pan and half-fill with water. Cook in the oven for 30–35 minutes or until the mixture is risen and firm to the touch. Serve hot.

MIXED CHEESE WITH HERBS

175 g / 6 oz curd cheese
25 g / 1 oz Gruyère cheese, grated
25 g / 1 oz Parmesan cheese, grated
pinch of mustard powder
salt and freshly ground black pepper

pinch of cayenne pepper
4–6 tablespoons chopped burnet or chervil

SERVES 4

Mash the soft cheese until smooth, then beat in the two grated hard cheeses. Add a pinch of mustard and season with salt and black pepper. Stir in a pinch of cayenne pepper, then chill for 2 hours until firm.

Form the cheese into balls and roll each one in the chopped herb. Lay them on a small flat plate and serve with warm water biscuits. *Illustrated on pages 82–3.*

SPINACH RAMEKINS

YOGURT CHEESE WITH DRIED HERBS

600 ml / 1 pint plain unsweetened yogurt
freshly ground black pepper
2 teaspoons olive oil
1 teaspoon sesame seeds
1 teaspoon dried thyme

SERVES 4
Low Fat

Served with rye bread or any good wholemeal bread and a Tomato and fennel salad (page 38), this makes a delicious light meal.

Line a colander or strainer with muslin and stand it over a bowl. Tip the yogurt into the muslin and tie it up with string, to form a bag. Lift it out of the colander. Tie the strings to a tap over a sink and leave to drain overnight.

The next day, tip the drained curds into a bowl and beat until smooth, adding a little salt and pepper and the olive oil. Form into a flat round shape.

Dry-fry the sesame seeds for about 1 minute until lightly browned, shaking the pan frequently. Set aside.

Pound the dried thyme and sesame seeds together in a mortar, then tip them on to a piece of greaseproof paper. Lay the cheese on the paper, turning it over so that it is coated all over with the pounded herbs. Chill in the refrigerator before serving.

LEFT: YOGURT CHEESE WITH DRIED HERBS; CENTRE: YOGURT DIP WITH FRESH HERBS (PAGE 84); RIGHT: MIXED CHEESE WITH HERBS (PAGE 81)

YOGURT DIP WITH FRESH HERBS

600 ml / 1 pint plain unsweetened yogurt
salt and freshly ground black pepper
¼ garlic clove, peeled and crushed
½ tablespoon chopped tarragon
½ tablespoon chopped dill
½ tablespoon chopped chervil or parsley

SERVES 4
Low Fat

Line a colander or strainer with muslin and stand it over a bowl. Tip the yogurt into the muslin and tie it up with string so that it forms a bag. Lift it out of the colander and leave it to drain overnight, tying the string to a tap over a sink.

The next day, tip the drained curds from the bag into a bowl. Beat until smooth, adding a little salt and pepper. Add the garlic and stir it in with most of the chopped herbs, reserving some to scatter over the top.

Pile the mixture into a small dish, level off with a palette knife, and sprinkle the remaining herbs on top. Chill for 1–2 hours before serving. *Illustrated on pages 82–3.*

HUMMUS

225 g / 8 oz chick peas, soaked overnight in cold
*   water and drained*
1 onion, peeled and roughly chopped
1 bay leaf
juice of 1 lemon
2 garlic cloves, peeled and crushed
2 tablespoons vegetable oil
300 ml / ½ pint plain unsweetened yogurt

½ teaspoon ground cumin seed
salt
TO GARNISH
chopped fresh parsley
black olives

SERVES 8–10
Low Fat   High Fibre

It is best to cook chick peas without using salt as this tends to toughen them if added at the beginning of the cooking time. Hummus is best made at least 24 hours in advance because it thickens on keeping.

Put the chick peas into a pan and cover with fresh water. Add the onion and bay leaf, then bring to the boil. Lower the heat, cover and cook for 1–1½ hours, or until chick peas are tender. Drain thoroughly, then remove the bay leaf.

Purée the peas and onion and mix in the lemon juice, garlic, oil, yogurt and cumin to make a fairly soft consistency. Season with salt.

Chill the hummus thoroughly, then garnish with parsley and black olives and serve with warm wholemeal pitta bread.

CHEESE AND MUSHROOM FONDUE

½ garlic clove, peeled
150 ml/¼ pint dry cider
1 teaspoon lemon juice
400 g/14 oz Gouda cheese, grated
1 tablespoon cornflour
1½ tablespoons gin, whisky, brandy or sherry

freshly ground white pepper
pinch of grated nutmeg
100 g/4 oz button mushrooms, trimmed and
    chopped

SERVES 6–8

Rub the inside of a flameproof earthenware casserole with the cut garlic, then chop a little of it and put into the casserole. Pour in the cider and lemon juice. Heat slowly until the cider is nearly boiling.

Gradually add the grated cheese, a little at a time, stirring constantly with a fork, until all the cheese has melted. When the mixture is boiling, blend the cornflour with the gin (or alternative spirit) until smooth, and stir into the fondue. Season with pepper and nutmeg, add the mushrooms and mix well.

Serve the fondue in the earthenware casserole with a bowl of French bread cubes. The cubed bread is speared with a long fork and dipped into the fondue.

VEGETABLE TERRINE

450 g/1 lb spinach, trimmed
4 tomatoes, thinly sliced
350 g/12 oz potatoes, peeled and coarsely grated
100 g/4 oz mushrooms, trimmed and finely
    chopped
1 onion, peeled and grated
50 g/2 oz Cheddar cheese, grated

2 tablespoons mixed fresh herbs, finely chopped
2 eggs
2 tablespoons skimmed milk
salt and freshly ground black pepper

SERVES 4
High Fibre

If fresh spinach is unavailable, 225 g/8 oz frozen spinach can be used. Cook as instructed on the packet, then drain and continue as in the recipe.

Cook the spinach with a minimum of water until soft. Drain thoroughly, chop and set aside.

Heat the oven to moderate (180°C, 350°F, Gas Mark 4). Grease the base and sides of a 900 ml (1½ pint) soufflé dish and cover with the tomato slices, retaining a few.

Mix together the potatoes, spinach, mushrooms, onion, cheese and herbs, then beat in the eggs and milk. Season with salt and pepper. Turn the mixture into the prepared dish and arrange the remaining tomato slices on top. Cover with foil or a lid and cook in the oven for 1½ hours. Leave to cool overnight, then turn out and serve in wedges.

Desserts

PINEAPPLE SORBET

1 × 1.5 kg (3 lb) pineapple
finely grated rind and juice of 1 large lemon
sugar to taste
2 egg whites

SERVES 6–8
Low Fat

Cut the pineapple in half lengthways, leaving the green leaves attached. Scoop out the pineapple flesh and discard the central core. Reserve the pineapple shells for serving. Alternatively, slice the top off the pineapple and scoop out the flesh.

Work the pineapple flesh to a purée with the orange rind and juice in a blender. Add sugar to taste. Transfer the purée to a bowl, then place in the freezer, or freezing compartment of the refrigerator, and freeze until half-frozen and beginning to thicken.

Beat the egg whites until stiff. Beat the half-frozen mixture well to break down the ice crystals, then fold in the beaten egg whites. Spoon the mixture into the pineapple shells and return to the freezer or freezing compartment. If there is too much mixture to fill the shells, freeze in a separate container.

To serve, allow the sorbet to soften slightly at room temperature for 10–15 minutes, or in the refrigerator for 20 minutes.

GERANIUM LEAF SORBET

12 scented geranium leaves
75 g / 3 oz caster sugar
300 ml / ½ pint water
juice of 1 large lemon
1 egg white

TO DECORATE
4 tiny geranium leaves

SERVES 4
Low Fat

Wash the geranium leaves and shake them dry. Put the sugar and water in a pan and boil until the sugar has dissolved. Put the leaves in the pan, cover it and turn off the heat. Leave for 20 minutes, then taste. If the flavour is too weak, bring the liquid to the boil once more, turn off the heat, cover the pan and leave it for a further 10 minutes.

When the flavour is satisfactory, strain the syrup into a rigid container, add the lemon juice and leave to cool. Freeze until semi-frozen, about 45 minutes–1 hour, then fold in the stiffly beaten egg white. Continue to freeze until a firm mush, about 1 hour. Serve in four glasses, each one decorated with a tiny geranium leaf.

BLACKCURRANT AND ORANGE ICE CREAM

225 g/8 oz blackcurrants, stalks removed
finely grated rind and juice of 1 orange
6–8 mint leaves
4 tablespoons soft brown sugar
300 ml/½ pint plain unsweetened yogurt
2 eggs, separated

TO DECORATE
4–6 small mint sprigs

SERVES 4–6
Low Fat   High Fibre

Put the blackcurrants into a blender, reserving a few for decoration. Add the orange rind and juice, the mint leaves, sugar, yogurt and egg yolks and blend until smooth.

Transfer the purée to a bowl, then place in the freezer, or freezing compartment of the refrigerator, and freeze until half-frozen and beginning to thicken.

Beat the egg whites until stiff, then fold into the ice cream. Freeze until half-frozen,

then beat again to prevent large ice crystals forming, then freeze until firm.

To serve, allow the ice cream to soften slightly at room temperature for about 10 minutes, or in the refrigerator for 20 minutes. Spoon into individual dishes or glasses, then decorate with the reserved blackcurrants and the mint sprigs.

RASPBERRY CHANTILLY

25 g/1 oz flaked almonds
450 g/1 lb raspberries, cleaned
2 tablespoons Grand Marnier or other liqueur
2 egg whites
100 ml/3½ fl oz plain unsweetened yogurt
grated rind of ½ lemon
1 tablespoon caster sugar

SERVES 4
High Fibre

Dry-fry the almonds for about 1 minute until lightly browned, shaking the pan frequently. Set aside. Put the raspberries into four glasses and spoon over the liqueur.

Just before serving, beat the egg whites

until stiff. Fold in the yogurt carefully with the lemon rind and sugar. Spoon over the raspberries and sprinkle with the almonds.

RHUBARB, ORANGE AND GINGER FOOL

450 g/1 lb rhubarb, trimmed and chopped
1 teaspoon bicarbonate of soda
finely grated rind and juice of 1 orange
3 tablespoons light soft brown sugar
150 ml/¼ pint skimmed milk
1 egg, lightly beaten
1 tablespoon cornflour

¼ teaspoon vanilla essence
150 ml/¼ pint plain unsweetened yogurt
1 tablespoon finely chopped preserved ginger
TO DECORATE
few orange slices

SERVES 4

Put the rhubarb and bicarbonate of soda in a saucepan, cover with water and bring to the boil. Strain and return the rhubarb to the rinsed pan with the orange rind and juice and the brown sugar. Cover and simmer gently for 10–15 minutes until tender. Mash the rhubarb to a pulp by beating vigorously with a wooden spoon, or purée in a blender. Leave to cool.

Heat the milk to just below boiling point. Put the egg in a bowl with the cornflour and vanilla essence. Beat lightly, then gradually stir in the hot milk. Pour the mixture back into the pan and bring to the boil slowly, stirring constantly. Cook, stirring, until the custard thickens.

Leave to cool, stirring occasionally to prevent a skin forming, then whisk in the yogurt. Stir the custard into the rhubarb purée with the ginger.

Spoon into a large serving bowl or four individual dishes or glasses. Chill in the refrigerator, then decorate with orange slices before serving. Serve chilled.

STRAWBERRY CRÈME CARAMEL

600 ml / 1 pint skimmed milk
4 eggs, beaten
225 g / 8 oz strawberries, hulled and halved
TOPPING
50 g / 2 oz demerara sugar

SERVES 4

Heat the oven to moderate (160°C, 325°F, Gas Mark 3).

Warm the milk in a saucepan over a low heat. Mix the beaten eggs with the warmed milk and pour into a 1.2 litre (2 pint) soufflé dish. Add the strawberries, cover the dish with foil and place in a small roasting pan, half-filled with water.

Bake in the oven for 1¼ hours or until set. Allow to cool completely.

Sprinkle the surface with demerara sugar and place under a hot grill until the sugar has caramelized. Serve immediately.

CHEESECAKE

75 g / 3 oz Strudel paste (page 107)
2 teaspoons oil
FILLING
175 g / 6 oz curd or sieved cottage cheese
1 egg, separated
1 teaspoon lemon juice
50 g / 2 oz caster sugar

1½ tablespoons plain flour
2 tablespoons plain unsweetened yogurt
50 g / 2 oz sultanas
icing sugar

SERVES 6
Low Fat

Preheat the oven to moderate (160°C, 325°F, Gas Mark 3).

Cut three 25 cm (10 inch) squares of Strudel paste. Brush each lightly with oil. Press evenly over the bottom and sides of an oiled, fluted flan dish 18–20 cm (7–8 inch) round. Turn over the surplus paste into the flan dish to make a neat edge and brush well with the remaining oil.

Soften the cheese in a large mixing bowl. Beat in the egg yolk, lemon juice, caster sugar, flour and yogurt. Fold in the sultanas. Whisk the egg white until stiff. Fold lightly but thoroughly into the cheese mixture. Spoon the mixture into the prepared tin and smooth the surface.

Bake in the oven for 30–40 minutes or until firm but still spongy to the touch. Sprinkle with a little icing sugar and serve at once.

WHOLEMEAL PROFITEROLES

150 ml / ¼ pint water
40 g / 1½ oz polyunsaturated margarine
65 g / 2½ oz wholemeal flour
2 small eggs
FILLING AND SAUCE
2 tablespoons cornflour
4 tablespoons cocoa powder

450 ml / ¾ pint skimmed milk
2 teaspoons sugar, or to taste
2 teaspoons instant coffee
1 egg, beaten

MAKES 24 profiteroles

The profiteroles can be made 1–2 days in advance and stored in an airtight tin. Should they need to be refreshed before using, stand them on a baking sheet in a preheated moderate oven (180°C, 350°F, Gas Mark 4) for about 5 minutes. Leave to cool on a wire tray before filling.

Put the water in a pan with the margarine and heat gently until the fat has melted. Bring to the boil and, when bubbling vigorously, remove from the heat and immediately add all the flour. Beat quickly with a wooden spoon until the mixture forms a ball and draws away from the sides of the pan.

Leave the mixture to cool slightly, then beat in the eggs a little at a time until the mixture is smooth and glossy. Put the mixture into a piping bag fitted with a 1.25 cm (½ inch) plain nozzle and pipe about twenty-four small rounds on to a lightly greased baking sheet. Space the rounds well apart to allow for expansion during the cooking. Bake just above the centre of a preheated hot oven (220°C, 425°F, Gas Mark 7) for 15–20 minutes.

To make the filling and sauce, whisk the cornflour and cocoa powder in a bowl with about a quarter of the milk. Heat the remaining milk with the sugar. Pour the hot milk over the ingredients in the bowl and return these to the pan. Bring to the boil, stirring constantly. Lower the heat and cook for a further few minutes.

Divide the mixture in half. Sprinkle the instant coffee into one half and keep warm. Add the egg to the other half of the mixture and stir over a low heat until it thickens, but ensure it does not overcook. Cool. Fill the buns with the cold egg mixture. Arrange in a bowl and cover with the warm coffee/chocolate sauce.

SPICED FRUIT COMPÔTE

450 g / 1 lb mixed dried fruit (apples, apricots, figs, peaches, pears, prunes, sultanas)
300 ml / ½ pint orange juice
300 ml / ½ pint water
1 cinnamon stick
2 cloves
50 g / 2 oz blanched slivered almonds

SERVES 4–6
Low Fat   High Fibre   Vegan

Put the dried fruit into a bowl and pour over the orange juice and water. Add the spices and leave to soak overnight. Alternatively, pour over boiling juice and water and soak for a few hours.

Transfer to a pan and bring to the boil. Lower the heat, cover and simmer for about 20 minutes or until the fruit is tender, adding more water if the syrup becomes absorbed.

Sprinkle with the almonds and serve warm or cold.

RED CURRANT SNOW WITH MINT

RED CURRANT SNOW WITH MINT

2 egg whites
300 ml / ½ pint plain unsweetened yogurt
2 tablespoons caster sugar
450 g / 1 lb red currants, washed and stalks
  removed
2 tablespoons chopped mint

SERVES 4
Low Fat   High Fibre

Beat the egg whites until they form stiff peaks. Beat the yogurt until it is smooth. Mix the egg whites with the yogurt, folding them together lightly with a metal spoon. Stir in the sugar. Fold the red currants into the yogurt. Stir in the chopped mint and serve soon after making.

VARIATION
Use blueberries instead of red currants.

LEMON FLUMMERY

300 ml / ½ pint water
25 g / 1 oz polyunsaturated margarine
grated rind and juice of 1 lemon
25 g / 1 oz plain flour

50 g / 2 oz caster sugar
1 egg, separated

SERVES 4

Place the water, margarine and lemon rind in a saucepan and bring to the boil, stirring to melt the fat. Mix the flour and sugar in a bowl. Gradually stir in the hot liquid. Add a little of this mixture to the egg yolk and mix well, then stir into the remaining mixture. Return to the saucepan and cook gently for 5 minutes, stirring frequently.

Pour the mixture into a bowl and stir in the lemon juice. Beat the egg white until stiff and fold into the mixture. Serve hot or cold with fruit.

FROSTED ALMOND CREAMS

2 eggs, separated
50 g / 2 oz soft brown sugar
50 g / 2 oz chopped almonds, toasted
300 ml / ½ pint plain unsweetened yogurt
2 tablespoons Grand Marnier or other liqueur

TO DECORATE
25 g / 1 oz toasted slivered almonds

SERVES 6

Beat the egg yolks and sugar together until thick and creamy. Stir in the chopped almonds, yogurt and liqueur. Beat the egg whites until just stiff, then fold into the almond mixture. Pour into six individual ramekin dishes and freeze until firm.

To serve, remove from the freezer and leave to soften slightly at room temperature for 15 minutes, or in the refrigerator for 30 minutes. Sprinkle with slivered almonds before serving.

LYCHEE AND ORANGE SALAD

6 oranges
1 × 300 g (11 oz) can lychees

SERVES 6–8
Low Fat   High Fibre   Vegan

For this recipe you need two plastic bowls: one about 15 cm (6 inch) and the other 20 cm (8 inch) in diameter.

Fill the large bowl half-full with water and place the smaller bowl inside, weighted to prevent it bobbing about. Adjust the weight, so that the ice 'bowl' will be about 2.5 cm (1 inch) thick at the bottom and 1 cm (½ inch) lower than the rim of the large bowl. Secure the rims with tape to keep the small bowl centred and freeze overnight.

The next day, peel away the skin and the pith of the oranges and divide into segments. Mix the oranges in a bowl with the lychees and their syrup. Keep cool.

Remove the ice 'bowl' from the freezer and let it stand for 10–15 minutes at room temperature. Do not place under hot or cold water or the ice 'bowl' will crack.

Remove the plastic bowls (they should slip off) and place the ice 'bowl' on a serving dish. Transfer the fruit salad to the ice 'bowl' and serve immediately.

SUNSHINE FRUIT SALAD

juice of 2 large oranges
juice of 1 lemon
2 tablespoons Cointreau, Grand Marnier or
  other liqueur (optional)
225 g/8 oz strawberries, hulled and halved
2 large peaches, halved, stoned and sliced

2 large bananas, peeled and sliced
2 passion fruit or pomegranates, halved

SERVES 4
Low Fat   High Fibre   Vegan

Put the orange and lemon juices into a serving bowl, then stir in the liqueur, if using. Add the strawberries.

Scoop out the flesh of the passion fruit or pomegranates with the seeds. Add the prepared fruit to the strawberries with the peaches and bananas and fold gently to coat with the juice. Serve chilled.

SUMMER PUDDING

750 g/1½ lb mixed berry fruit (loganberries,
  blackcurrants, red currants, blackberries,
  strawberries, raspberries)
150 ml/¼ pint water
50 g/2 oz caster sugar
8 slices slightly stale wholemeal bread, crusts
  removed

TO DECORATE
150 ml/¼ pint plain unsweetened yogurt
  (optional)

SERVES 6
Low Fat   High Fibre
Vegan (if decoration omitted)

Put the fruit and water into a heavy pan with the sugar and cook gently for 10 minutes. If using strawberries or raspberries, add them after the rest of the fruit has been cooked to prevent their disintegrating.

Strain the fruit, reserving the cooking juice.

Cut a circle from one of the slices of bread to line the base of a 900 ml (1½ pint) pudding basin. Cut sufficient wedges of bread to line the sides of the basin, reserving any scraps to fill gaps in the bread lining.

Dip each piece of this bread into the reserved juice and line the basin. Fill with half the fruit, place another layer of bread on top, then spoon in the rest of the fruit and top with another layer of bread. Spoon over any remaining fruit juice.

Put a plate that just fits inside the basin's rim on the pudding and put several heavy weights on top. Chill overnight.

Place a sieve over a bowl and line with muslin. Pour in the yogurt and leave to drain for about 3 hours until most of the liquid has drained through, leaving the yogurt in the sieve with a smooth, creamy consistency.

To serve, turn the pudding on to a dish and spoon or pipe yogurt, if liked, on top to decorate.

VARIATION
The balance of the fruits can be varied. Make a Spring pudding by adding some tender stewed rhubarb with the early soft fruits, or add a higher proportion of stewed blackberries and dessert apple to make an Autumn pudding.

PEARS IN CASSIS

300 ml / ½ pint white wine
100 g / 4 oz blackcurrants, stalks removed
2 tablespoons honey
1 cinnamon stick
2 strips lemon rind
4–6 dessert pears, peeled but leaving stalks
  attached
1 teaspoon arrowroot

SERVES 4–6
Low Fat   High Fibre   Vegan

Pour the wine into a pan, then add the blackcurrants, honey, cinnamon and lemon rind. Heat gently until the honey has dissolved, then bring to the boil. Boil for 1 minute.

Put the pears in the pan, submerging them as much as possible in the wine mixture. Cover and cook gently for about 20 minutes until the pears are tender, turning occasionally.

Lift the pears carefully out of the pan and transfer to a serving bowl. Discard the cinnamon stick and lemon rind.

Blend the arrowroot with a little cold water, then pour into the wine mixture. Bring to the boil, then lower the heat and simmer for 1 minute until the sauce thickens, stirring constantly. Pour over the pears. Serve hot or cold.

APRICOT SYLLABUB

225 g / 8 oz dried apricots
600 ml / 1 pint water
finely grated rind and juice of 1 lemon
150 ml / ¼ pint plain unsweetened yogurt
2 tablespoons Grand Marnier or other liqueur
50 g / 2 oz soft brown sugar
2 egg whites

TO DECORATE
lemon twists or chopped nuts

SERVES 6
Low Fat (if nuts omitted)
High Fibre

Put the apricots into a bowl, pour over the water, then add the lemon rind and juice. Leave to soak overnight. Alternatively, pour over boiling water and soak for a few hours.

Transfer to a pan and bring to the boil. Lower the heat, cover and simmer for 20–30 minutes until the apricots are soft, adding more water if necessary.

Work the mixture to a smooth purée in a blender, then transfer to a bowl and leave to cool.

Stir the yogurt, liqueur and sugar into the purée until well blended. Beat the egg whites until just stiff, then fold into the mixture.

Spoon into a serving bowl or six individual dishes or glasses, then chill in the refrigerator for at least 1 hour before serving. Decorate with lemon twists or nuts.

PLUM AND ORANGE COBBLER

450 g/1 lb Victoria plums
juice of 2 oranges
1 orange, peel and pith removed and divided
  into segments
2 tablespoons caster sugar
TOPPING
225 g/8 oz wholemeal flour
1 teaspoon ground mixed spice
2 teaspoons baking powder
½ teaspoon salt

25 g/1 oz polyunsaturated margarine
25 g/1 oz soft brown sugar
finely grated rind of 1 orange
150 ml/¼ pint plain unsweetened yogurt or
  skimmed milk
skimmed milk or beaten egg to glaze

SERVES 4
Low Fat   High Fibre

Preheat the oven to hot (220°C, 425°F, Gas Mark 7).

Place the plums in a baking dish. Add the orange juice and segments and sprinkle over the sugar.

To make the topping, put the flour, spice, baking powder and salt in a bowl and stir well. Rub in the margarine, then stir in the sugar and orange rind. Add the yogurt or milk and mix to a soft dough.

Turn the dough out on to a lightly floured surface and roll out to about 1 cm (½ inch) thickness. Cut out 8–10 rounds with a 4 cm (1½ inch) pastry cutter, then arrange overlapping around the edge of the dish. Brush with a little milk or beaten egg.

Bake in the oven for about 15 minutes until the topping is risen and brown and the plums are just tender when pierced with a skewer. Serve hot.

APPLE STRUDEL

DOUGH
75 g/3 oz Strudel (page 107) or filo paste
  sufficient to make two 25 cm/10 inch squares
FILLING
275 g/10 oz cooking apples, peeled, cored and
  coarsely grated
25 g/1 oz raisins
25 g/1 oz currants
25 g/1 oz caster sugar

¼ teaspoon ground cinnamon
2 teaspoons finely grated lemon rind
1 teaspoon vegetable oil
TO DECORATE
icing sugar, sieved

SERVES 4
Low Fat

Warm a rolling pin, and flour a large clean teatowel. Roll the dough on the towel according to the instructions on page 107, then leave it to rest for 15 minutes, covered with a damp cloth. Mix all the filling ingredients together and spread on the dough to within 2.5 cm (1 inch) of the edges. Brush the edges with a little water. Lift the two corners of the teatowel nearest to you and roll the dough away from you.

Pinch the edges of the strudel to seal. Place the dough on a greased baking sheet and form into a horseshoe. Brush all over with the oil. Bake in a moderately hot oven (200°C, 400°F, Gas Mark 6) for about 20 minutes, then reduce the temperature to 180°C, 350°F, Gas Mark 4 for a further 30 minutes. Serve warm or cold. Dust with icing sugar, cut into slices, and serve with plain unsweetened yogurt, if liked.

BLACKBERRY AND APPLE COBBLER

BLACKBERRY AND APPLE COBBLER

*750 g / 1½ lb cooking apples, peeled, cored and
  sliced*
1–2 tablespoons granulated sugar
4 tablespoons water
225 g / 8 oz blackberries, cleaned
TOPPING
225 g / 8 oz wholemeal flour
pinch of salt

2 teaspoons baking powder
25 g / 1 oz polyunsaturated margarine
25 g / 1 oz caster sugar
150 ml / ¼ pint skimmed milk
skimmed milk to glaze

SERVES 4
Low Fat   High Fibre

Heat the oven to hot (220°C, 425°F, Gas Mark 7) and place a shelf near the top.

Put the apples into a saucepan with the sugar and water. Poach until softened, then add the blackberries and cook for a further 3 minutes.

Pour the cooked fruit into a 1.2 litre (2 pint) ovenproof pie dish.

To make the topping, put the flour, baking powder and salt together into a bowl and rub in the fat, until the mixture resembles fine breadcrumbs. Stir in the sugar and enough milk to bind the mixture together. (It should not be wet.)

Turn the dough on to a lightly floured board and roll out to a thickness of 1 cm (½ inch). Cut out rounds with a 4 cm (1½ inch) fluted cutter.

Arrange the scone rounds overlapping round the edge of the pie dish and glaze with a little milk.

Bake in the oven for 10–15 minutes until the topping is golden brown.

VARIATION
Try using cooked fruits such as plums, gooseberries, apples and raspberries, or apricots.

BLACK PEAR PUDDING

4 pears, peeled, cored and sliced
100 g/4 oz blackberries, cleaned
finely grated rind and juice of 1 lemon
75 g/3 oz soft brown sugar
50 g/2 oz polyunsaturated margarine
1 large egg, beaten
100 g/4 oz plain wholemeal flour

1 teaspoon ground cinnamon
2 teaspoons baking powder
1 tablespoon skimmed milk

SERVES 4
High Fibre

Heat the oven to moderate (180°C, 350°F, Gas Mark 4).

Put the pears and blackberries into a 900 ml (1½ pint) ovenproof pie dish. Sprinkle over the lemon rind and juice and 2 tablespoons of the sugar.

Cream the margarine and remaining sugar together until pale and fluffy. Beat in the egg with a little of the wholemeal flour and the cinnamon.

Fold in the remaining flour and baking powder with the milk to give a soft dropping consistency, then spread the mixture over the fruit and level the surface.

Bake in the oven for 45 minutes until the topping is risen and brown. Serve hot.

CHERRY CUSTARD PUDDING

350 g/12 oz cherries, stoned
50 g/2 oz polyunsaturated margarine
25 g/1 oz caster sugar
finely grated rind and juice of 1 large lemon
2 eggs, separated
300 ml/½ pint skimmed milk

50 g/2 oz self-raising wholemeal flour
½ teaspoon ground cinnamon

SERVES 4
High Fibre

Heat the oven to moderate (180°C, 350°F, Gas Mark 4).

Put the cherries into a greased ovenproof dish.

Cream together the margarine, sugar and lemon rind until pale and fluffy. Beat in the egg yolks a little at a time, then stir in the milk, lemon juice, flour and cinnamon to give a loose, curd-like mixture.

Beat the egg whites until just stiff, then fold into the mixture and spoon on top of the cherries.

Place the dish in a roasting pan, half filled with hot water. Bake in the oven for 40–45 minutes until the top is set, firm and golden. (The pudding will have separated to give a layer of cherries and custard with a sponge topping.) Serve hot.

GOOSEBERRY CRUMBLE

450 g/1 lb gooseberries, topped and tailed
2 tablespoons caster sugar
juice of 1 orange
CRUMBLE
100 g/4 oz wholemeal flour or rolled oats
50 g/2 oz margarine

50 g/2 oz soft brown sugar
finely grated rind of 1 orange

SERVES 4
High Fibre   Vegan

Heat the oven to moderately hot (200°C, 400°F, Gas Mark 6). Put the gooseberries into a 900 ml (1½ pint) ovenproof pie dish. Sprinkle over the sugar, then pour over the orange juice.

To make the crumble, put the flour in a bowl, then rub in the margarine. Stir in the brown sugar and reserved orange rind, then spoon on top of the gooseberries to cover them completely.

Bake in the oven for 30 minutes until the crumble is crisp and brown. Serve hot.

HAZELNUT AND RASPBERRY TORTE

TORTE
4 eggs, separated
100 g/4 oz soft brown sugar
100 g/4 oz shelled hazelnuts, coarsely ground
FILLING
450 g/1 lb dessert apples, peeled, cored and sliced
finely grated rind and juice of ½ lemon

225 g/8 oz raspberries, cleaned
TO DECORATE
150 ml/¼ pint plain unsweetened yogurt
few whole hazelnuts
few raspberries (optional)

SERVES 6–8
High Fibre

Heat the oven to moderate (180°C, 350°F, Gas Mark 3).

To make the torte, beat the egg yolks and sugar together until thick and creamy. Beat the egg whites until just stiff. Fold the ground hazelnuts and egg whites carefully into the creamed mixture.

Grease and base line two 23 cm (9 inch) sandwich tins with greased greaseproof paper or non-stick silicone paper. Divide the mixture equally between the tins and level the surface.

Bake in the oven for 30 minutes until risen and firm to the touch. Leave in the tins until cold. Do not turn out on to a wire tray or the cakes will stick.

To make the filling, put the sliced apples into a pan with the lemon rind and juice, and raspberries. Cook for 10–15 minutes until pulpy, stirring occasionally. Remove from the heat and beat until smooth, or rub through a sieve for a smoother texture. Leave to cool.

Meanwhile, place a sieve over a bowl and line with a piece of muslin. Pour in the yogurt and leave to drain for about 3 hours until most of the liquid has drained through, leaving the yogurt with a smooth, creamy consistency in the sieve.

To assemble the torte, lift the cooled cakes carefully out of the tins and peel off the paper. Place one cake on a serving plate and spread with the filling mixture. Cover with the other cake, then pipe the creamy yogurt in rosettes on the top. Decorate with whole hazelnuts. (Alternatively, the top may be lightly dusted with icing sugar and decorated with raspberries or raspberry leaves.)

Baking

CHAPPATIS

225 g/8 oz wholemeal flour
pinch of salt
about 150 ml/¼ pint water
margarine for spreading

MAKES 8 chappatis
Low Fat   High Fibre
Vegan (without margarine)

Sift the flour and salt into a large bowl and make a hollow in the centre. Add the water gradually, working in the flour to make a firm dough. Knead well for about 15 minutes, until the dough is smooth. Cover with a damp cloth and leave to stand for about 30 minutes. The dough should be quite firm and hard. Divide the dough into eight portions. Roll each into a circle, about 15 cm (6 inch) in diameter, sprinkl-ing the rolling pin and work surface with flour to prevent sticking.

Cook each chappati in a very hot heavy frying pan, without fat. When the top surface shows signs of bubbling, turn the chappati over and cook for 30–40 seconds on the other side. Then place the chappati under a warm grill until it puffs up. Spread margarine lightly on one side, fold over and serve hot.

PURIS

100 g/4 oz wholemeal flour
100 g/4 oz plain flour
½ teaspoon salt
25 g/1 oz polyunsaturated margarine, melted
about 150 ml/¼ pint water
oil for deep frying

MAKES 8 puris
High Fibre

Sift the dry ingredients into a large bowl and return bran in the sieve to the bowl. Make a hollow in the centre and pour in the melted margarine. Add the water grad-ually, kneading the mixture, until a firm dough is formed. Continue to knead for a further 5–10 minutes. Cover with a damp cloth and leave to stand for 15 minutes.

Divide the dough into eight pieces and roll each into a thin circle 10–13 cm (4–5 inch) in diameter.

Heat the oil to hot and fry the puris, one at a time. After a few seconds the puris will puff up. Press down with a fish slice or the back of a spoon. When the puris are crisp and golden, remove from the oil and drain on absorbent kitchen paper. Serve hot.

VARIATION
To make cocktail puris, break off small pieces of dough and roll into circles 4 cm (1½ inch) in diameter. As soon as they are cooked, sprinkle with sesame salt or celery salt.

TOP: CHAPPATIS; BOTTOM: PURIS

SWEDISH FLAT BREAD

225 g/8 oz stone ground wholemeal flour
225 g/8 oz rye or barley flour
1 teaspoon salt
250–350 ml/8–12 fl oz tepid water

MAKES 4 crispbreads
Low Fat   High Fibre

Blend the flours together with the salt. Mix in sufficient water to bind into a dough – the quantity will depend on the types of flour used. Beat until the dough leaves the sides of the bowl, then turn on to a floured board and knead thoroughly. Heat a griddle or frying pan over a moderate heat and grease it. Divide the dough into four and roll out one quarter into a round as thin as possible. Using a plate about 20 cm (8 inch)

wide, trim the edges into a neat circle. Prick all over to prevent the dough bubbling during cooking.

Transfer to the griddle or frying pan and cook over a moderate heat for about 15 minutes or until slightly coloured, then turn and cook the other side. Repeat with the rest of the dough, working up the trimmings for re-rolling and baking. Cool on a wire tray.

OATMEAL PLAIT

2 teaspoons caster sugar
150 ml/¼ pint skimmed milk heated to 50°C,
*   110°F*
150 ml/¼ pint water heated to 50°C, 110°F
1½ teaspoons dried yeast
400 g/14 oz strong plain white flour
1 teaspoon salt
25 g/1 oz polyunsaturated margarine

100 g/4 oz fine or medium oatmeal
skimmed milk or water to glaze
little coarse oatmeal

MAKES 2 smaller plaits or 1 cob loaf or
10–12 rolls
Low Fat

Smaller plaits are baked for 20–25 minutes and rolls for 15–20 minutes. If wished, use fresh instead of dried yeast (see page 103).

To make the dough, dissolve 1 teaspoon of the sugar in the milk and water and blend the yeast into it. Leave in a warm place for 10–15 minutes, until the surface is covered with bubbles.

Sift the flour, salt and the remaining sugar into a bowl, rub in the margarine, then mix in the oatmeal. Add the yeast liquid and mix to form a fairly soft dough. Turn out on to a floured surface and knead for 10 minutes or until smooth and no longer sticky (or for 3–4 minutes in an electric mixer fitted with a dough hook). Shape dough into a ball, place in an oiled polythene bag and tie loosely. Leave to rise in a warm place for about 1 hour, until doubled in size.

Grease a baking sheet. Remove the dough from the bag, knock back and knead for about 2 minutes or until smooth. Divide into three equal pieces. Roll into three sausage shapes, all the same length and about 4 cm (1½ inch) in diameter.

Lay the lengths close to each other and, beginning in the middle, plait towards you. Pinch the ends together to secure them. Turn the plait round and complete the plait, again securing the ends.

Place on the baking sheet, brush with milk or water and sprinkle with coarse oatmeal. Cover with a sheet of oiled polythene and leave to rise in a warm place until doubled in size. Meanwhile, heat the oven to hot (230°C, 450°F, Gas Mark 8).

When the dough has doubled, bake in the oven for 25–35 minutes or until well risen and lightly browned and it sounds hollow when the base is tapped.

BASIC BROWN OR WHITE BREAD

15 g/½ oz dried yeast
2 tablespoons soft brown sugar
900 ml/1½ pints water heated to 50°C, 110°F
1 tablespoon salt
1.5 kg/3 lb wholemeal or strong white flour
25 g/1 oz polyunsaturated margarine
1 egg, beaten with a pinch of salt

MAKES 1 × 1 kg (2 lb) loaf and 2 × 450 g (1 lb) loaves or
1 × 1 kg (2 lb) loaf and about 40 rolls
Low Fat

Fresh yeast may be used in place of dried – 25 g/1 oz fresh yeast is equivalent to 15 g/½ oz dried yeast. If using fresh yeast, dissolve it in the liquid – no sugar is needed. Make sure when dissolving yeast that the liquid is heated to 50°C, 110°F; if it is too cool, the dough will not rise properly.

Put the dried yeast into a small bowl with 1 teaspoon of the sugar and whisk in 300 ml/½ pint of the water. Leave in a warm place for 10–15 minutes, until the surface is covered with bubbles.

Add the salt and the remaining sugar to the rest of the water. Either of the following two methods may be used for mixing the dough:

1 Put the flour into a large bowl and rub in the margarine. Pour in both the salted water and the yeast liquid. Quickly work the flour and liquid together to a dough with the fingertips. If the mixture seems dry, add a little more water. Knead the dough for 5 minutes until smooth, pulling the outside dough into the centre.

2 Using an electric mixer, put the flour into the mixer bowl with the butter, salt water and yeast liquid. Mix on a slow speed, using the dough hook attachment, until the liquid is absorbed. Continue mixing for 2 minutes, instead of kneading by hand.

Put the kneaded dough into a greased bowl and cover with a damp cloth. Leave in a warm place for about 45 minutes. The dough should double in size.

Turn out the risen dough on a floured working surface and knead lightly, using as little flour as possible. The dough is now ready for shaping.

LOAVES

Warm and grease a 1 kg (2 lb) loaf tin. Halve the dough and keep one half warm. Knead the other portion into a smooth ball and punch into a shape to fit the prepared loaf tin.

Warm and grease two 450 g (1 lb) loaf tins. Halve the remaining dough and shape to fit the two tins. Brush the loaves with the beaten egg mixture. If using a wholemeal dough, sprinkle with a little cracked wheat or bran.

Cover with polythene bags and leave to rise in a warm place for 20 minutes until the dough reaches the top of the tins.

Meanwhile, heat the oven to hot (230°C, 450°F, Gas Mark 8).

Bake the loaves in the oven for 20 minutes, then reduce the temperature to moderately hot (200°C, 400°F, Gas Mark 6) for a further 20 minutes for the large loaf, and 10 minutes for the smaller loaves. Tip the loaves out of their tins and tap them on the bottom – the loaves should sound hollow if they are cooked. Cool on a wire tray.

ROLLS

Grease baking sheets. Divide the dough into 50 g/2 oz portions; this amount will make about 40 rolls. Roll under a cupped hand on a lightly floured surface until round and smooth. Arrange on the prepared baking sheets and brush with a little beaten egg mixture. They can be sprinkled with sesame, poppy or caraway seeds, or bran. Cover with polythene bags and leave in a warm place to rise for 10–5 minutes. Meanwhile, heat the oven to hot (230, 450°F, Gas Mark 8). Bake the rolls for 10–15 minutes. *Illustrated on pages 104–5.*

RYE BREAD

25 g / 1 oz dried yeast
2 tablespoons black treacle
900 ml / 1½ pints water
1 tablespoon salt
1 kg / 2 lb wholemeal flour
450 g / 1 lb rye flour

25 g / 1 oz polyunsaturated margarine
1 egg, beaten with a pinch of salt
cracked wheat or bran

MAKES 2 loaves
Low Fat   High Fibre

To make the rye bread dough, put the yeast into a small bowl with the black treacle, then follow the same method as for Basic brown or white bread (page 103), using the mixed wholemeal and rye flours in place of the wholemeal or white flour. Allow the dough to rise for 45 minutes and then knead lightly.

Heat the oven to hot (230°C, 450°F, Gas Mark 8). Grease two baking sheets.

Halve the risen dough and shape each portion into a long, oval loaf. Place the shaped loaves on the prepared baking sheets, brush the surface with the beaten egg mixture and sprinkle with cracked wheat or bran.

Make several diagonal cuts in the surface of the loaves with a sharp knife. These cuts allow the loaves to rise or 'bloom' well, hence the name 'bloomer'. Bake for 20 minutes, then reduce the temperature to moderately hot (200°C, 400°F, Gas Mark 6) for a further 20 minutes.

OATCAKES

100 g / 4 oz medium oatmeal
½ teaspoon salt
pinch of bicarbonate of soda
2 teaspoons vegetable oil
about 50 ml / 2 fl oz hot water

MAKES 4 thick or 6 thin 'farls'
Low Fat   Vegan

Mix the oatmeal, salt and bicarbonate of soda in a bowl. Make a well in the centre, pour in the oil and add enough water to make a stiff dough which can be squeezed into a ball. Sprinkle the board and your hands with oatmeal and knead the mixture until there are no cracks. Flatten the ball and roll it out into a round just under 5 mm (¼ inch) thick. Invert a plate on top and trim off the ragged edges. (Work up the trimmings and roll out and add them to the next batch of dough.)

Cut the round 'bannock' across into four triangles, called 'farls'. With a palette knife lift them on to a warmed and greased griddle or thick-based frying pan and cook over a moderate heat for 20 minutes or until the farls curl at the corners. Turn and cook the other side for 5 minutes or finish under a preheated moderate grill.

Store the oatcakes in an airtight tin and toast under a moderate grill or in the oven before serving.

If you prefer very thin oatcakes, make a slightly softer dough and roll it out as thin as possible. Trim the bannock and cut it into six farls. The thin oatcakes will cook more quickly and need care in handling.

CHOCOLATE BISCUITS

50 g / 2 oz polyunsaturated margarine
100 g / 4 oz plain wholemeal flour
3 tablespoons cocoa powder
50 g / 2 oz caster sugar
1 tablespoon skimmed milk

MAKES 14 biscuits

Preheat the oven to moderately hot (190°C, 375°F, Gas Mark 5).

Rub the margarine into the flour. Add the cocoa and sugar. Using a knife, mix all together with the milk. Knead to a smooth ball and roll on a floured board. Cut into rounds with a 6 cm (2½ inch) pastry cutter and place on a greased baking sheet.

Bake in the oven for 15 minutes and cool on a wire tray.

DOUGHS FOR BASIC BROWN AND WHITE BREADS (PAGE 103) AND A SELECTION OF BREADS AND ROLLS MADE FROM THEM

WHOLEMEAL TREACLE SCONES

100 g/4 oz plain flour
100 g/4 oz plain wholemeal flour
25 g/1 oz caster sugar
½ teaspoon cream of tartar
½ teaspoon bicarbonate of soda
1 teaspoon ground mixed spice

50 g/2 oz polyunsaturated margarine
2 tablespoons black treacle, warmed
7 tablespoons skimmed milk

MAKES 10–12 scones

Heat the oven to moderately hot (190°C, 375°F, Gas Mark 5).

Put the dry ingredients into a bowl and stir until thoroughly mixed. Rub in the margarine, then stir in the warmed treacle and the milk.

Turn the dough out on a floured surface and knead lightly. Roll out gently until about 1 cm (½ inch) thick and stamp out about ten rounds with a 5 cm (2 inch) cutter.

Place the scones on a greased and floured baking sheet and brush with remaining milk. Bake in the oven for 20 minutes. These scones should be served very fresh.

WHOLEMEAL PANCAKES

50 g/2 oz plain wholemeal flour
½ teaspoon baking powder
150 ml/¼ pint skimmed milk
1 egg white
vegetable oil for frying

MAKES 4 pancakes
Low Fat   High Fibre

Sieve the flour and baking powder into a basin and return the bran in the sieve to the flour. Whisk in the milk gradually. Beat the egg white until it is stiff but not dry and fold into the batter. Brush a 20 cm (8 inch) non-stick frying pan with a little oil. Pour in a quarter of the batter and tilt the pan to coat the bottom evenly with the batter.

Cook until the underside is brown, then turn over and cook for 10 seconds. Remove and repeat with the remaining batter to make four pancakes, stacking the pancakes between lightly oiled foil as they are cooked.

WHOLEMEAL SHORTCRUST PASTRY

75 g/3 oz wholemeal flour
40 g/1½ oz polyunsaturated margarine
50 g/2 oz cold mashed potato
1 tablespoons ice-cold water

MAKES sufficient to line 1 × 20 cm (8 inch) flan ring

Put the flour in a bowl. Add the margarine and rub into the flour until the mixture resembles breadcrumbs. Stir in the potato and then the water. Kneed to a firm dough.

Turn on to a lightly floured surface, roll out and use according to the recipe.

STRUDEL PASTE

225 g / 8 oz plain flour
½ teaspoon salt
1 large egg, lightly beaten
2 tablespoons vegetable oil
3 tablespoons tepid water

MAKES 225 g / 8 oz of dough
Low Fat

Sieve together the flour and salt. Make a well in the centre and pour in the egg and oil. Add the water gradually, stirring with a fork, to make a soft sticky dough. Work the dough in the bowl until it leaves the sides clean, then turn out on to a lightly-floured surface and knead for about 15 minutes or until the dough feels smooth and elastic. Form into a ball, place in a bowl and cover with a warm cloth. Leave to rest for 1 hour.

Warm the rolling pin, and flour a large clean teatowel. Place the dough on the towel and roll it out to a rectangle as thinly as possible, lifting and turning it to prevent it from sticking to the cloth. Using the backs of your hands, gently stretch the dough, working from the centre to the outside until it is paper thin – you should be able to read through the dough, but to do this takes years of practice and patience. Leave the dough to rest for 15 minutes before using.

FRUIT MALT LOAF

225 g / 8 oz wholemeal flour
100 g / 4 oz sultanas
2 tablespoons vegetable oil
50 g / 2 oz malt extract
25 g / 1 oz black treacle
25 g / 1 oz fresh yeast

5 tablespoons tepid water
1 tablespoon clear honey, to glaze

MAKES 1 × 450 g (1 lb) loaf
Low Fat   High Fibre   Vegan

Put the flour and sultanas into a warm bowl and mix well.

Put the oil, malt extract and black treacle into a pan and heat gently. Leave to cool for 5 minutes.

Blend the yeast with the water, then add to the dry ingredients with the contents of the pan and mix to a soft dough. Turn out on to a lightly floured surface and knead for 5 minutes until smooth. Place the dough in a warmed, greased bowl. Cover and leave in a warm place for about 1 hour until doubled in size.

Warm a 450 g (1 lb) loaf tin and brush lightly with oil. Heat the oven to moderately hot (200°C, 400°F, Gas Mark 6).

Turn the risen dough out on to a floured surface and knead again for 5 minutes. Fold the dough into three, then place in the loaf tin. Cover with a clean damp cloth and leave in a warm place for about 20 minutes until the dough rises to the top of the tin.

Bake in the oven for 45 minutes. Turn out on to a wire tray, brush with honey, then leave to cool.

SPICY APPLE, DATE AND SESAME LOAF

350 g/12 oz self-raising wholemeal flour
¼ teaspoon fine salt
¼ teaspoon grated nutmeg
1 teaspoon ground mixed spice, or ¼ teaspoon
*   ground allspice, ¼ teaspoon ground mace, ¼*
*   teaspoon ground cardamom and ¼ teaspoon*
*   ground ginger*
1 teaspoon ground cinnamon
grated rind of ½ lemon

50 g/2 oz muscovado sugar
2 eggs, beaten
150 ml/¼ pint plain unsweetened yogurt
1 large cooking apple, peeled, cored and grated
225 g/8 oz stoned dates, chopped
50 g/2 oz sesame seeds

MAKES 1 × 1 kg (2 lb) loaf
Low Fat   High Fibre

Heat the oven to moderate (160°C, 325°F, Gas Mark 3). Grease and lightly flour a 1 kg (2 lb) loaf tin.

Sift the flour, salt and spices into a large bowl, tipping in any bran left in the sieve. Stir in the lemon rind and sugar and make a well in the centre. Pour in the eggs and yogurt and gradually mix the dry ingredients into the liquid. Stir in the apple, dates and 25 g/1 oz of the sesame seeds.

Shape the mixture into a loaf and put into the prepared loaf tin. Press the mixture down in the corners and smooth the top with the back of a spoon. Scatter over the rest of the sesame seeds and press them into the top of the loaf.

Bake in the oven for 1½–1¾ hours until well-risen and lightly browned. Allow the loaf to cool in the tin for 5–10 minutes before turning it out on to a wire tray to cool completely. Store for at least 1 day before serving.

VARIATIONS
For 100 g/4 oz of the dates, substitute 100 g/4 oz glacé cherries, chopped, or 100 g/4 oz walnuts, chopped.

ORANGE, CARROT AND NUT CAKE

100 g/4 oz polyunsaturated margarine
100 g/4 oz caster sugar
1 teaspoon ground cinnamon
1 teaspoon grated orange rind
2 eggs, lightly beaten
75 g/3 oz raw carrot, finely grated
50 g/2 oz shelled walnuts, finely chopped

1 tablespoon orange juice
225 g/8 oz self-raising wholemeal flour
1 teaspoon baking powder

MAKES 1 × 20 cm (8 inch) cake
High Fibre

This cake improves in flavour if kept for at least one day before cutting.

Heat the oven to moderate (180°C, 350°F, Gas Mark 4). Grease and line a 20 cm (8 inch) cake tin with greaseproof paper and grease the paper.

Cream the margarine and sugar together in a bowl until pale and fluffy. Beat in the ground cinnamon and orange rind. Gradually add the eggs, beating well after each

addition. Stir in the grated carrot, chopped nuts and orange juice. Mix the flour and baking powder together and fold into the creamed mixture.

Turn into the prepared cake tin and smooth the top. Bake in the oven for 45–55 minutes, or until the centre of the cake springs back when lightly pressed with a fingertip. Turn out on a wire tray to cool.

BANANA CAKE

100 g/4 oz self-raising wholemeal flour
100 g/4 oz polyunsaturated margarine
50 g/2 oz muscovado sugar
2 eggs, beaten
2 ripe bananas, peeled and mashed
½ teaspoon baking powder
a little icing sugar, to finish
FILLING
225 g/8 oz low-fat curd cheese

½ teaspoon lemon juice
about 1 tablespoon thick honey
1 large banana, peeled and sliced

**MAKES 1 × 18 cm (7 inch) round
sandwich cake
High Fibre**

Heat the oven to moderate (180°C, 350°F, Gas Mark 4). Grease and line two 18 cm (7 inch) sandwich tins with greaseproof paper. Grease the paper.

Sift the flour into a bowl, tipping in any bran left in the sieve. Set aside. Cream the margarine with the sugar in another bowl until the mixture is fluffy. Beat in the eggs a little at a time, adding 1 tablespoon of the sifted flour after each addition. Fold in the rest of the flour with a metal spoon.

Combine the mashed bananas with the baking powder, then fold into the cake mixture. Mix thoroughly, but do not beat as this would remove the air already incorporated and might make the cake crack.

Divide the mixture between the sandwich tins and smooth the tops. Bake in the preheated oven for 30–40 minutes, or until the cakes are springy to the touch. Cool on a wire tray.

To make the filling, beat together the cheese, lemon juice and honey. Spread this over one cake layer, then peel and slice the banana and arrange on the filling. Cover with the other cake layer and dust lightly with sifted icing sugar.

If you want to make and fill the cake in advance, keep it in the refrigerator, or bake the cake and store it in an airtight container until required, then spread with the filling just before serving.

COUNTRY FRUIT CAKE

250 g/9 oz self-raising wholemeal flour
½ teaspoon ground mixed spice
½ teaspoon bicarbonate of soda
75 g/3 oz polyunsaturated margarine
75 g/3 oz caster sugar
100 g/4 oz raisins
100 g/4 oz sultanas
25 g/1 oz peeled and grated apple

25 g/1 oz mixed peel
1 egg, beaten
175 ml/6 fl oz skimmed milk
5 sugar cubes

**MAKES 1 × 15 cm (6 inch) round cake
High Fibre**

Grease and line a 15 cm (6 inch) round cake tin, or a 22 × 11 × 6 cm (8½ × 4½ × 2½ inch) loaf tin, and heat the oven to moderate (180°C, 350°F, Gas Mark 4).

Sift the flour, spices and bicarbonate of soda together into a large bowl. Return the bran remaining in the sieve to the flour. Rub in the margarine. Stir in the sugar, dried fruit, grated apple and mixed peel. Pour in the beaten egg and mix well. Stir in

the milk to give the mixture a soft consistency.

Spoon the mixture into the prepared cake tin. Roughly crush the sugar cubes with the end of a rolling pin and scatter them over the cake. Bake in the centre of the oven for about 1–1¼ hours until golden brown.

Cool slightly before turning out on to a wire tray.

Packed Meals

COTTAGE PEARS

175 g/6 oz cottage cheese
50 g/2 oz blue Brie cheese, rinded and chopped
25 g/1 oz walnuts, chopped
salt and freshly ground black pepper

4 ripe dessert pears, peeled, quartered and cored
juice of ½ lemon

SERVES 4

Mix together the cottage cheese, Brie and walnuts, reserving 3 teaspoons, salt and pepper until well blended.

Slice the pear quarters thinly and brush immediately with the lemon juice.

Spread some cottage cheese on top of the pears. Repeat the process with another layer of pears and cottage cheese and sprinkle with some of the nuts.

Carefully pack the pears in a tight-lidded container.

ONION QUICHE

1 × 20 cm (8 inch) Wholemeal shortcrust pastry
  flan case (page 106)
FILLING
25 g/1 oz polyunsaturated margarine
750 g/1½ lb large onions, peeled and thinly
  sliced

3 eggs
250 ml/8 fl oz skimmed milk
salt and freshly ground black pepper

SERVES 4
High Fibre

Heat the oven to hot (220°C, 425°F, Gas Mark 7).

Melt the margarine in a heavy saucepan and gently cook the onions until they start to soften.

Beat together the eggs and milk, and season with salt and pepper. Stir in the onions and pour the mixture into the flan case. Bake in the oven for 20–25 minutes until the filling is set and golden.

SPINACH TIMBALE

4 eggs
300 ml/½ pint skimmed milk
225 g/8 oz frozen, chopped spinach, thawed
50 g/2 oz fresh wholemeal breadcrumbs
50 g/2 oz Cheddar cheese, grated

¼ teaspoon grated nutmeg
salt and freshly ground black pepper

SERVES 4
High Fibre

This dish may also be served hot with Fresh tomato sauce (page 52) as a light main course at home.

Grease a 1.5 litre (2½ pint) ovenproof ring mould and heat the oven to moderate (180°C, 350°F, Gas Mark 4).

Beat the eggs and the milk together in a bowl. Stir in the spinach, breadcrumbs, cheese and nutmeg. Season with salt and pepper and pour into the prepared dish. Bake in the oven for about 1 hour (exact time depends on the depth of the dish) until the custard is set and slightly risen. Test with a skewer, which should come out clean.

Leave in the dish and cool before covering with cling film for packing.

VEGETABLE PÂTÉ

450 g/1 lb courgettes, grated
1 tablespoon coarse salt
15 g/½ oz polyunsaturated margarine
1 small onion, peeled and grated or finely
 chopped
3 garlic cloves, peeled and crushed
2 eggs
150 ml/¼ pint skimmed milk
½ tablespoon herb mustard
2 tablespoons chopped mixed fresh herbs (e.g.
 chervil, chives, mint, parsley)

freshly ground black pepper
large pinch of cayenne pepper
225 g/8 oz fresh spinach, rinsed and drained
TO GARNISH
8 tablespoons shredded white cabbage
2 large carrots, scrubbed and grated
1 medium tomato
few chives

SERVES 6–8
Low Fat

If you are short of time, you can omit the spinach, which makes a striking dark green covering for the pâté.

Put the courgettes into a colander and sprinkle them with the coarse salt. Leave to drain for 30 minutes. Rinse the courgettes under cold running water, then drain again.

Meanwhile, line a well-greased 1 kg (2 lb) loaf tin with non-stick silicone paper and preheat the oven to moderate (180°C, 350°F, Gas Mark 4).

Melt the margarine in a non-stick frying pan, add the onion and garlic and fry over a moderate heat for 3 minutes, stirring occasionally. Add the courgettes, stir well and cook gently for 10 minutes, stirring once or twice. Remove the pan from the heat and leave to cool.

Beat the eggs and milk together. Stir in the cooled vegetables, the mustard and herbs and season to taste with pepper and cayenne – it should not be too bland.

Pour the mixture into the prepared tin and cover the tin with foil. Stand the tin in a roasting tin and pour in about 4 cm (1½ inch) of cold water.

Cook in the oven for 30 minutes. Leave the pâté to cool in the tin.

Strip the stalks from the spinach leaves. Place the spinach in a large saucepan of boiling salted water, cover and cook for 2 minutes. Drain the leaves, and pat dry.

Turn the pâté out on to a dish and peel off the lining paper. Arrange the drained spinach leaves in an attractive pattern on top of the pâté. The pâté may now be packed in a rigid, lidded container.

Skin the tomato and make 8 equidistant incisions through it from the top, stopping short of the base. Peel the cut sections back gently and remove the inner pith and seeds. Pack the tomato with the other garnish ingredients in a lidded container.

When the pâté is unpacked and placed on a dish, spread the cabbage and carrot round it. Invert the tomato on top of the pâté and decorate with chives to resemble stalks.

PASTA SALAD

25 g/1 oz blanched almonds
100 g/4 oz mixed coloured pasta shells or twists
3 tablespoons vegetable oil
100 g/4 oz peas, fresh or frozen
3 celery sticks, chopped
1 small bunch spring onions, chopped
6 black olives, stoned and chopped

1 tablespoon wine vinegar
salt and freshly ground black pepper
TO GARNISH
watercress sprigs

SERVES 4
High Fibre

Toast the almonds: dry-fry for about 1 minute until lightly browned, shaking the pan frequently.

Cook the pasta and fresh peas in boiling salted water with 1 tablespoon of the oil for about 10 minutes, or until tender. If using frozen peas, add them halfway through the cooking time.

Drain well and run cold water through the pasta pieces to keep them separate. Leave to cool.

Put the celery into a bowl with the pasta and peas. Add the spring onions, olives and almonds.

Mix the remaining oil with the vinegar and season with salt and pepper. Pour over the pasta salad and toss all the ingredients together. Pack the salad into a lidded container and garnish with watercress sprigs.

TOMATO QUICHE

1 × 20 cm (8 inch) Wholemeal shortcrust pastry
   case (page 106)
FILLING
350 g/12 oz tomatoes, skinned and thinly sliced
1 small onion, peeled and chopped
1 teaspoon chopped basil
1 teaspoon chopped parsley
1 teaspoon thyme
2 tablespoons boiling water

salt and freshly ground black pepper
1 egg
250 ml/8 fl oz skimmed milk
TO GARNISH
tomato slices
parsley

SERVES 4
High Fibre

Heat the oven to moderate (180°C, 350°F, Gas Mark 4).

To make the filling, put the tomatoes, onion, basil, parsley, thyme and water in a saucepan and season with salt and pepper. Simmer for 5–6 minutes or until the vegetables are soft, then cool.

Beat together the egg and milk, then add to the tomato mixture. Pour into the flan case and bake in the oven for 35–40 minutes until the filling is set and golden. Garnish with the tomato and parsley.

LEFT: PASTA SALAD; RIGHT: TOMATO QUICHE

Slimmers' Recipes

BAKED POTATOES

Potatoes should not be ruled out when dieting. They are both nutritious and satisfying and, with a filling, can make a balanced meal.

Choose even-sized potatoes, if cooking more than one.

Scrub and dry the potatoes, then prick all over with a fork. Place on a baking sheet and bake in a preheated hot oven (200°C, 400°F, Gas Mark 6) for 1–1¼ hours until tender when pierced with a knife.

Serve with any one of the following fillings.

BLUE CHEESE FILLING

50 g/2 oz Danish blue cheese, crumbled
4 teaspoons plain unsweetened yogurt
salt and freshly ground black pepper

FOR 1 potato

Combine the cheese with the yogurt and season with salt and pepper to taste.

Cut a cross in the top of each potato and spoon on the cheese and yogurt mixture.

Return to the oven for 2 minutes to heat through. *Illustrated on page 116.*

COTTAGE CHEESE FILLING

50 g/2 oz cottage cheese
2 teaspoons tomato purée
salt and freshly ground black pepper

FOR 1 potato
Low Fat

Mix the cottage cheese and tomato purée and season with salt and pepper to taste.

Cut the potato in half, scoop out the flesh and combine with the cheese mixture.

Spoon back into the potato shells and return to the oven for 2 minutes to heat through. *Illustrated on page 116.*

CAMEMBERT FILLING

50 g/2 oz Camembert cheese, rinded
50 g/2 oz cottage cheese
salt and freshly ground black pepper

FOR 1 potato

Mash the Camembert with the cottage cheese and season with salt and pepper to taste.

Cut the potato in half, scoop out the flesh and combine with the cheese mixture.

Spoon back into the potato shells. Place under a heated grill for 2 minutes to heat through. *Illustrated on page 116.*

MEDITERRANEAN LENTIL STEW

2 teaspoons vegetable oil
2 onions, peeled and chopped
1 garlic clove, peeled and crushed
2 celery sticks, trimmed and sliced
4 small courgettes, trimmed and sliced
4 tomatoes, skinned and quartered
900 ml/1½ pints water or stock
¼ teaspoon ground coriander

salt and freshly ground black pepper
225 g/8 oz brown lentils
TO GARNISH
2 tablespoons chopped parsley

SERVES 4
Low Fat   High Fibre   Vegan

Heat the oil in a large pan and gently cook the onions, garlic, celery and courgettes for 10 minutes until lightly browned, stirring frequently.

Add the tomatoes, water or stock, coriander and salt and pepper to taste. Bring to the boil and add the lentils, then cover and simmer for 1–1½ hours until the lentils are tender.

Sprinkle with the chopped parsley, if liked, and serve hot.

If preferred, the dish can be cooked in the oven. Brown the vegetables in a flameproof casserole, add the remaining ingredients, cover and cook in a preheated moderate oven (180°C, 350°F, Gas Mark 4) for 1½–2 hours. Sprinkle with parsley and serve. *Illustrated on page 72.*

HARICOT BEAN PAPRIKA

350 g/12 oz haricot beans, soaked overnight in
    cold water
2 teaspoons vegetable oil
1 large onion, peeled and sliced
1 garlic clove, peeled and crushed
1 tablespoon paprika
salt

2 tablespoons tomato purée
50 g/2 oz canned pimento, sliced
1 × 400 g (14 oz) can tomatoes
150 ml/¼ pint water

SERVES 4
Low Fat   High Fibre   Vegan

Drain the beans, cover with fresh water and bring to the boil. Cook for 45 minutes or until almost tender, then drain.

Meanwhile, heat the oil in a large non-stick pan and gently cook the onion and garlic until soft. Stir in the paprika, season with salt and cook, stirring, for 2–3 minutes. Add the beans, tomato purée, pimento, tomatoes and water.

Bring to the boil, cover and simmer gently for about 10 minutes.

CRUDITÉS

6 small green peppers, cored, seeded and sliced
   into strips
1 large red pepper, cored, seeded and sliced into
   strips
1 large yellow pepper, cored, seeded and sliced
   into strips
1 bunch celery (white part only), trimmed,
   separated into sticks and halved
2 fennel bulbs (white part only), trimmed and
   cut into strips

2 cucumbers, thinly sliced
1 bunch radishes, topped and tailed
450 g/1 lb young, tender, broad beans
8 small violet-coloured artichokes, stalks, outer
   leaves and chokes removed

SERVES 8
Low Fat High Fibre

Arrange the prepared vegetables attractively on a large platter or in a basket, mixing the colours as much as possible – they look pretty arranged in the shape of a flower. The artichokes must be immersed in a bowl of water to which a few drops of lemon juice have been added or they will discolour. Serve as soon as possible after preparing the vegetables, with a choice of dips, such as Cottage cheese dip or Yogurt dip (page 118).

LEFT: BAKED POTATOES WITH COTTAGE CHEESE, CAMEMBERT AND BLUE CHEESE FILLINGS (PAGES 114–15)

ABOVE: MINTED GRAPEFRUIT (PAGE 119)

COTTAGE CHEESE DIP

450 g / 1 lb cottage cheese
1 teaspoon caraway seeds
½ green pepper, cored, seeded and finely
  chopped
2 tablespoons finely chopped watercress
½ teaspoon salt
freshly ground black pepper

1 garlic clove, crushed (optional)
TO GARNISH
½ teaspoon paprika

SERVES 10–12
Low Fat

If a smoother dip is preferred, sieve the cottage cheese.

Blend together the cottage cheese, caraway seeds, green pepper, watercress, salt, pepper and garlic, if used. Pile the dip into a bowl and sprinkle with paprika.

YOGURT DIP

150 ml / ¼ pint plain unsweetened yogurt
225 g / 8 oz cottage cheese
1 tablespoon grated onion
6 pickled gherkins, very finely chopped
1 teaspoon salt

SERVES 4–6
Low Fat

Thoroughly mix the yogurt, cottage cheese, onion and gherkins in a bowl and stir well to mix. Chill in the refrigerator for 1 hour. Transfer to a serving bowl.

CABBAGE FLAN

750 g / 1½ lb cabbage (spring, summer, primo or
  Savoy), trimmed
salt and freshly ground black pepper
2 eggs, beaten
150 ml / ¼ pint plain unsweetened yogurt

50 g / 2 oz Cheddar cheese, grated
large pinch of grated nutmeg

SERVES 4–6
Low Fat

Heat the oven to moderately hot (190°C, 350°F, Gas Mark 5). Grease a 20 cm (8 inch) flan dish.

Remove the outside leaves of the cabbage and shred the heart finely. Place the large leaves in a pan of boiling, salted water with the shredded cabbage on top and cook for 5 minutes. Drain well, then separate the large leaves from the shredded cabbage and remove the thick parts of the stems.

Line the base and sides of the prepared flan dish with 6–8 of the outside leaves, pressing them firmly into place.

Mix together the eggs, shredded cabbage, yogurt and cheese and season with salt and pepper. Pour the filling into the lined dish and sprinkle the nutmeg over the surface.

Cook in the oven for 25–30 minutes or until the filling is set. The leaves around the edge may need to be brushed with a little oil during the cooking time so that they do not dry out.

BAKED YOGURT CUSTARD

300 ml / ½ pint plain unsweetened yogurt
few drops of vanilla essence
2 eggs, beaten
150 ml / ¼ pint skimmed milk
¼ teaspoon grated nutmeg

SERVES 4
Low Fat

Heat the oven to moderate (170°C, 325°F, Gas Mark 3).

Put the yogurt and vanilla into a bowl and mix well. Add the eggs and milk and beat well to an even colour.

Pour into an ovenproof dish and sprinkle with the nutmeg.

Stand the dish in a roasting pan and pour in enough water to come 2.5 cm (1 inch) up the sides of the pan. Bake in the oven for 40 minutes. Serve hot or cold with fresh or stewed fruit.

MINTED GRAPEFRUIT

2 large grapefruit
2 oranges
1 tablespoon lemon juice
1 × 250 ml (8 fl oz) bottle low-calorie lemonade
2 tablespoons finely chopped fresh mint

TO DECORATE
4 mint sprigs

SERVES 4
Low Fat   Vegan

Halve the grapefruit, using a zig-zag cut. Remove the flesh from the halves. Peel and segment the oranges, remove the membranes and cut the segments into pieces. Mix with the grapefruit and return to the grapefruit shells.

Mix together the lemon juice, lemonade and chopped mint. Pour into an ice tray and freeze until mushy. Pile on top of the grapefruit and decorate with a sprig of mint. Serve immediately. *Illustrated on page 117.*

Cooking For Two

FLORENTINE CROWNS

2 slices wholemeal bread
polyunsaturated margarine to spread
100 g/4 oz cooked leaf spinach, drained and
    chopped
50 g/2 oz Mozzarella cheese, diced
2 large eggs, separated
salt and freshly ground black pepper

TO GARNISH
watercress

SERVES 2
High Fibre

Heat the oven to moderate (180°C, 350°F, Gas Mark 4).

Toast the bread and spread lightly with margarine, then cover each slice with the spinach and Mozzarella.

Season the egg whites with salt and pepper and whisk until soft peaks form. Pile half the egg white on to each slice of toast. Make a hollow in the centre and slip the yolk into the hollow. Place on a baking sheet and cook in the oven for about 10 minutes until browned and the yolk is set. Serve immediately, garnished with watercress.

BROWN RICE WITH VEGETABLES

150 g/5 oz brown rice
600 ml/1 pint water or Vegetable stock (page
    20)
salt
1 bay leaf
1 tablespoon vegetable oil
1 garlic clove, peeled and crushed
1 onion, peeled and finely chopped
2 celery sticks, trimmed and thinly sliced
1 green pepper, cored, seeded and thinly sliced
1/2 teaspoon dried basil
50 g/2 oz mature Cheddar cheese, grated

freshly ground black pepper
2 large tomatoes, thinly sliced
TO GARNISH
chopped parsley

SERVES 2
High Fibre

LEFT: BROWN RICE WITH VEGETABLES;
RIGHT: FLORENTINE CROWNS

Put the rice into a colander and rinse in cold running water. Turn into a bowl, cover with cold water and allow to soak for 30 minutes. Drain and put into a pan with the water or stock, salt and bay leaf. Bring to the boil, then cover the pan and simmer over a gentle heat for 40–45 minutes, or until the rice is tender and the liquid absorbed.

Fifteen minutes before the rice is cooked, heat the oil in a large non-stick frying pan. Gently fry the garlic, onion, celery and green pepper until they are soft but not browned. Stir in the basil, half the cheese, and rice and season with pepper. Toss lightly with a fork until heated through.

Spoon the mixture into a shallow flameproof casserole dish and arrange the tomato slices on top. Sprinkle with the remainder of the grated cheese and place under a hot grill for 2–3 minutes until the cheese is golden and bubbly. Sprinkle with chopped parsley and serve.

MUFFIN PIZZAS

2 wholemeal muffins or baps
1 × 225 g (8 oz) can tomatoes, drained and
  chopped
8–10 black olives, stoned and chopped
1 small garlic clove, peeled and crushed
½ teaspoon dried oregano

salt and freshly ground black pepper
50 g/2 oz mature Cheddar cheese, grated

SERVES 2
High Fibre

Toast the muffins on both sides under the grill then split open. Put the tomatoes in a bowl and mix in the olives, garlic, and oregano. Season with salt. Spread evenly over the muffins, then top with the grated cheese.

Place under a medium hot grill until the cheese is bubbling. Serve immediately.

CORN AND BEAN DINNER

1 × 200 g (7 oz) can sweetcorn kernels, drained
225 g/8 oz cooked beans
1 × 225 g (8 oz) can tomatoes
1 medium onion, peeled and finely chopped
100 g/4 oz unsalted roasted peanuts, finely
  chopped

salt and freshly ground black pepper
100 g/4 oz mature Cheddar cheese, grated

SERVES 2
High Fibre

Grease a baking dish and heat the oven to moderate (180°C, 350°F, Gas Mark 4).

Mix together the corn, beans, tomatoes with their juice, onion and peanuts and season with salt and pepper. Spoon into the baking dish and sprinkle with the cheese. Cook in the oven for 30 minutes.

VEGETABLE LAYER

1 small aubergine, sliced
1 tablespoon vegetable oil
1 onion, peeled and sliced
1 large leek, sliced
3 courgettes, sliced
50 g/2 oz mature Cheddar cheese, grated

1 teaspoon dried oregano
salt and freshly ground black pepper
150 ml/¼ pint tomato juice

SERVES 2

Grease a 1.2 litre (2 pint) casserole dish and heat the oven to moderate (180°C, 350°F, Gas Mark 4).

Blanch the aubergine in boiling water for 2 minutes, drain and pat dry. Heat the oil in a pan and cook the aubergine and onion for 5 minutes.

Layer the aubergine and onion with the leek and courgettes in the casserole dish. Sprinkle each layer with cheese, oregano and salt and pepper. Pour over the tomato juice.

Cover tightly and cook in the oven for 45 minutes–1 hour or until the vegetables are tender.

Serve hot with boiled brown rice.

BANANAS RIO

2 medium-ripe bananas, peeled
3 tablespoons orange juice
1 tablespoon lemon juice
15 g / ½ oz polyunsaturated margarine
2 tablespoons demerara sugar

1 tablespoon freshly grated or desiccated coconut
plain unsweetened yogurt

SERVES 2

Lightly grease a shallow casserole and heat the oven to moderately hot (200°C, 400°F, Gas Mark 6).

Put the bananas in the dish. Combine the orange and lemon juices and pour them over the bananas. Dot with the margarine, sprinkle over the sugar and cook in the oven for 10–15 minutes.

Serve hot or warm, sprinkled with the coconut and topped with the yogurt.

APPLE CRISP

polyunsaturated margarine for spreading
2 slices wholemeal bread, crusts removed
15 g / ½ oz soft brown sugar
pinch of ground cinnamon

1 cooking apple, peeled, cored and thinly sliced
15 g / ½ oz polyunsaturated margarine

SERVES 2

Heat the oven to moderately hot (190°C, 375°F, Gas Mark 5).

Spread the bread lightly with margarine and arrange, fat-side down, in a shallow ovenproof dish. Mix the sugar and cinnamon and sprinkle half over the bread.

Arrange the apple slices on top and sprinkle with the rest of the spiced sugar. Dot with the margarine.

Cover the dish with lightly greased foil and cook in the oven for 25–30 minutes, until the bread is crisp and the apples soft. Serve with yogurt.

MEAL PLANS

The table of suggested daily intakes below gives a guide to how menus can be composed. The recommendations are sub-divided according to sex, as men require more calories than women. The choice of foods would yield between 30 and 34 per cent of total calories derived from fat. By carefully choosing from a wide variety of foods, the total fat intake could be lowered still more, or the proportion of unsaturated fats increased – for instance, soya products or nuts could be used instead of cheese.

The following meal plans are examples of how, by using the advice given in the introduction together with the suggested daily food allowances, you can create your own eating pattern for a healthier diet based on the recipes in this book.

SUGGESTED DAILY INTAKES

PRODUCT	MEN	WOMEN
Wholemeal bread	225 g / 8 oz	175 g / 6 oz
Cereals (rice, flour)	100 g / 4 oz	50 g / 2 oz
Breakfast cereals	50 g / 2 oz	50 g / 2 oz
Root vegetables	250 g / 9 oz	175 g / 6 oz
Green leafy vegetables★	2 portions	2 portions
Raw salad vegetables★	1 portion	1 portion
Fruits★ and fruit juice	4 portions	2 portions
Dried fruits★	1 portion	1 portion
Pulses (cooked)	250 g / 9 oz	175 g / 6 oz
Nuts, seeds, cheese and soya products	100 g / 4 oz	50 g / 2 oz
Semi-skimmed milk or enriched soya milk	300 ml / ½ pt	300 ml / ½ pt
or skimmed milk	600 ml / 1 pt	600 ml / 1 pt
Oil	30 ml / 2 tablespoons	15 ml / 1 tablespoon
Margarine	40 g / 1½ oz	25 g / 1 oz
Eggs	3–4 / week	3–4 / week

★ All portions of fruit and vegetables: about 100 g / 4 oz minimum.

VEGETARIAN

BREAKFAST
Fruit muesli with yogurt
wholemeal bread with
   polyunsaturated
   margarine
tea or coffee with skimmed
   milk

LIGHT MEAL
Hummus with wholemeal
   pitta bread
Watercress with orange and
   nuts
Cheesecake

MAIN MEAL
Vine-leaf parcels
Underground hotpot
Tossed green salad
wholemeal bread
Apricot syllabub

VEGAN

BREAKFAST
glass of fruit juice
Porridge with soya milk
Fruit malt loaf with
   margarine
tea or coffee with soya milk
   if desired

LIGHT MEAL
Italian bean soup
Oatcakes with margarine
Tomato and fennel salad
Spiced fruit compôte

MAIN MEAL
Tabbouleh with pitta bread
Lentil patties with Fresh
   tomato sauce
Herb risotto
Leeks Niçoise
Summer pudding

LOW CALORIE

BREAKFAST
Banana flip
1 slice wholemeal bread,
   toasted
low-fat spread
tea or coffee with skimmed
   milk

LIGHT MEAL
Yogurt cheese with herbs
Rye bread
Winter salad
1 slice of melon
coffee with skimmed milk

MAIN MEAL
Haricot beans paprika
Baked potato with
   Camembert filling
Cos lettuce with yogurt
   dressing
Minted grapefruit
coffee with skimmed milk

Daily total: 1125 calories

INDEX